Promoting
Academic
Success *for*
ESL Students

UNDERSTANDING
SECOND LANGUAGE ACQUISITION
FOR SCHOOL

by Virginia P. Collier, George Mason University

Published by
**New Jersey Teachers of English to Speakers of Other Languages-Bilingual Educators
(NJTESOL-BE)**

This is the first of a series of monographs intended to present recent scholarship in the field of Bilingual Education and English as a Second Language. As such, this publication is addressed to interested professionals in the field of education who are concerned with issues of language minority students.

NJTESOL-BE wishes to express appreciation to the administration of Jersey City State College for its active support of efforts represented by this monograph; and to Mr. Ronald Bogusz, Director of the Office of Publications and Special Programs at Jersey City State College, who designed this publication.

Published by NJTESOL-BE in cooperation with the Multicultural Center and with the Office of Publications and Special Programs at Jersey City State College, Jersey City, New Jersey 07305

For information on ordering additional copies, contact:

Bastos Educational Books
P.O. Box 770-433
Woodside, NY 11377
1-800-662-0301   FAX: 1-718-997-6445

Contents

Introduction

This is a no-nonsense, down-to-earth discussion of a very complex topic: academic second language acquisition, or how we learn a second language for school. The context of the discussion is education in the United States, for students of all ages. The students who are the center of attention in this monograph are studying English as a second language or have studied it sometime in their past. Some consider these students to be a big problem that they wish would somehow go away, while others delight in their presence and consider them special resources for our country. They include language minority students who are here to stay and international students who plan to return to their home countries. Language minority students (a federal government term) include recently arriving immigrants as well as eighth-generation citizens of the U.S. who speak languages other than English at home.

How did I get involved working with these students? As a child growing up in Greensboro, North Carolina, I spent a somewhat unusual childhood driving with my family to Mexico and Central America for long excursions so that my dad could conduct historical research in libraries and archives there. Growing up bilingually, I found myself between two worlds and later identified with the Central American immigrants settling in Washington, D.C., where I began my professional life as an ESL and bilingual social studies teacher, after having been a high school Spanish teacher. Experience as a teacher, school administrator and curriculum developer led me to pursue a doctorate specializing in second language acquisition and education. Now my goal is to translate research findings into useful applications for educators.

As I have worked with superintendents, administrators, school counselors, university faculty, adult educators, and K-12 teachers, I am continually amazed at the misinformation that persists about second language acquisition. One reason is that language issues are very emotional and quickly become political. But educators also can be gullible, relying on hunches, Grandpa's experiences, and wishful thinking, when there is so much that we actually know now from research findings.

This monograph is a dispersion of myths regarding how people learn languages. The information that I present here is based on a very deep knowledge base that was extremely scanty only 20 years ago. We know much more now about how we acquire language from research conducted not just in linguistics but in all the social sciences as well as in education. We still have lots to learn. But we know enough now that I have some very specific recommendations for educators.

Those who view language minority students as a problem should realize that they are with us to stay. Given this reality, it makes sense to assist these students with the best support that we can give them to help them be productive citizens. In the long run, all of us will benefit.

Language Acquisition: An Overview

As we examine the research findings, you may be surprised that young children are not the fastest to pick up a second language. Based on hundreds of studies examining the influence of age on second language acquisition, we now know that adolescents and young adults are the most efficient acquirers of second language. But there are other complicating factors that make it difficult to say that one age is better than another to begin a second language. Age of first exposure to the new language is an important issue that we will examine in some depth. The encouraging news is that people of all ages can efficiently acquire a second language.

The discouraging news is that learning a second language, even when efficient and occurring under the best of circumstances, is difficult and very complex for all ages. It takes a long time, and we must have great patience with the process. I am not just talking about using the language to carry on a conversation or buy food at the grocery store. Instead, developing full English proficiency means being able to use oral and written English in every aspect of adult life, including advanced schooling and all professional contexts. There is no way to speed up the natural, subconscious, developmental linguistic process, which is one aspect of language acquisition.

But there are ways to influence the two other major aspects: sociocultural and cognitive processes. The teacher can make a difference in the conscious cognitive processes that influence language acquisition. Sociocultural processes that influence second language acquisition can be changed through the context in which students are schooled. We will examine these three major dimensions of second language acquisition: linguistic, sociocultural, and cognitive processes in some detail within educational contexts.

Another myth dispelled by research of the past 20 years is the notion that first language "interferes" with second language. This was an idea popular among foreign language educators that never was substantiated by research. Certainly the two languages influence each other in many ways, but the research has found that first language plays a very positive and powerful role in the second language acquisition process. We will examine the relationship between a student's first and second languages within an education context.

One more myth I will mention here is the commonly held belief that ESL students need to be taught basic skills before they can move on to more complex tasks. Yet the research shows that an emphasis on basic skills is a sure way to slow down their progress in both English language development and in academics. Beginning ESL students can be taught cognitively complex tasks right from the start. Furthermore, they should not be held back in academic development just because they do not speak English. Both subject matter and English can be developed simultaneously. Likewise, some teachers still believe that students have to have an oral base before reading and writing can be introduced. This, too, is a myth. Research on literacy development shows clearly that learning is accelerated when all language skills are developed simultaneously.

In this monograph, we will address these and other myths by examining the three major dimensions of language acquisition—*linguistic, sociocultural, and cognitive processes—within educational contexts, for all ages of students.* I have chosen these organizers because they represent the overriding factors that influence second language development, according to the many theories developed in second language acquisition research over the past decade (Ellis, 1985;

Larsen-Freeman, 1985; Larsen-Freeman & Long, 1991; McLaughlin, 1987; Wong Fillmore, 1985, 1991b). In fact, in my own research analyzing key variables in second language acquisition for schooling, these three dimensions continue to surface as major overall influences.

I present this information in short form, designed to facilitate decision-making for educators. To guide the reader to sources that provide details of the many research studies that have been conducted on each topic that this monograph addresses, references are provided throughout the text. Most of these references do not represent simply one study, but instead they are syntheses of many studies addressing the points made in the text here. It is useful to remember that when examining studies of human behavior in social science and education research, one study tells us very little, but 50 well-designed studies that find similar results are worthy of our attention. Every point made here is backed up by many studies. I hope you will find the reading both interesting and thought-provoking.

Linguistic Processes

I am using the term "linguistic processes" to refer only to the subconscious aspects of language development. That is, these occur inside the learner's head. We educators have less influence on these processes. They are natural and universal. These aspects of language acquisition have been discovered mainly by linguists. They are important for educators to understand because sometimes we work in opposition to the natural language acquisition process and our well-meaning but misguided strategies in teaching may hold back student progress.

First Language Acquisition

To understand second language acquisition, you need to know a little bit about *first language acquisition.* How do we pick up our first language? Is it quick and easy? I wish I could say yes, but instead, it *is a complex, lifelong process.* All of our adult life we are learning new vocabulary, picking up new subtleties in pragmatics (the social context of language), and expanding our skills in writing. Language is constantly changing, and we monitor and absorb the changes that affect our everyday oral and written communication with others.

For young children, development of oral language is universal. Given no physical disabilities or no isolation from humans, all children of the world innately develop a full and complex oral language system (Berko Gleason, 1993; de Villiers & de Villiers, 1978). When a five-year-old English-speaking child first enters school, he/she has already subconsciously picked up listening and speaking skills in English phonology (pronunciation), vocabulary, grammar, semantics (meaning), and pragmatics (social context), at the cognitive level of a five-year-old. This is an incredible accomplishment. We often think of this level of language development as full proficiency, but the most gifted five-year-old is not yet half-way through the process of first language development.

Sometimes judgments of school personnel can be misguided at this stage. Too often teachers or special resource staff talk about a child having "no language" or "limited language," when what they really mean is that the child is not familiar with the standard variety used in school. Linguists analyzing each American English dialect and regional variety in depth have found that each language system used in a given community has a full grammar and vocabulary system equally as complex as the standard variety—just different. Accepting this difference means recognizing that the child's oral language system is full and complex, affirming the child's potential, and assisting with the process of bidialectal acquisition of the language of school.

Continuing the language acquisition process in school and at home, from ages 6 to 12, children both subconsciously and consciously absorb subtle phonological distinctions, vocabulary and semantic development, grammar rules, formal thought patterns, and complex aspects of pragmatics in the oral system of English (de Villiers & de Villiers, 1978; Goodluck, 1991; McLaughlin, 1984, 1985). Formal schooling adds reading and writing to the language skills of listening and speaking, taught across all the dimensions of language listed above. Still another layer of complexity is the increasing cognitive level of language use required with each age and grade level, for each subject area. An adolescent entering college still faces enormous amounts of new vocabulary to acquire in each discipline of study, as well as continuing acquisition of writing skills. By young adulthood, first language proficiency development is nothing short of a phenomenon, and yet we continue to increase our knowledge and uses of our native language throughout our lifetime. Language acquisition is an unending process (Berko Gleason, 1993; Collier, 1992a; Harley, Allen, Cummins & Swain, 1990; McLaughlin, 1985).

Second Language Acquisition

Likewise, *second language acquisition is a complex phenomenon, a lifelong process, with many parallels with first language acquisition.* From the first days of exposure to the new language, whatever our age, we use some of the same innate processes that are used to acquire our first language (Chomsky, 1964, 1965). We go through developmental stages similar to those in first language acquisition, making some of the same types of errors in grammatical markers that young children make, picking up chunks of language without knowing precisely what each word means, and relying on sources of input—humans who speak that language—to provide modified speech that we can at least partially comprehend (Ellis, 1985; Hakuta, 1986).

However, this remarkable ability to learn a second language that we innately possess is more subject to influences from other factors than was oral development in our first language. We will examine some of these major factors in the remainder of this monograph. Among the most influential factors in the natural, subconscious process, we will examine: the context in which the language will be used (which affects the level of proficiency required), the role of a student's first language, age differences, and the type of input needed for second language to flourish. First, we will take a brief look at the natural developmental process itself.

NATURAL DEVELOPMENTAL PROCESSES IN SECOND LANGUAGE ACQUISITION

The evidence for an innate process comes from research on the types of errors that students make as they go through increasing exposure to the second language. At first it was assumed that students' errors were mostly structures transferred from their first languages. Now there is substantial research evidence that *many error patterns are predictable across all learners, regardless of their first language or the formal instruction given to them in the second language* (Brown, 1994; Ellis, 1985; Hakuta, 1987; Krashen, 1981; Larsen-Freeman & Long, 1991).

For example, all ESL learners pass through a predictable sequence of stages while acquiring English negation, interrogation, and relative clauses, whatever their first language. In the first stage, most English learners develop a word order common to ESL learners that is different from standard English word order, with some sentence constituents omitted. In the second stage, the learner begins to use more standard English word order and most required sentence constituents are there (subject-verb), but grammatical accuracy is still missing. The third stage leads to more systematic and meaningful usage of grammar markers (although still with plenty of errors). In the fourth stage, more complex sentence structures are increasingly used by the English learner (Ellis, 1985, pp. 58-64). This all happens gradually with increasing exposure to the language. The rate at which learners reach each stage varies with each individual student. Likewise, the sequence of acquisition of specific structures of English varies from student to student. But understanding that *ESL students pass through general developmental stages common across all second language learners* can help teachers to have patience with the process.

It also helps to know that *the process is not linear.* Language acquisition is more like a zigzag process. One day you can feel immensely satisfied that a student seems to have mastered a particular grammar marker—or morpheme—but the next day in another context, the error shows up again. This is to be expected. Perhaps you are focusing on regular past tense (the morpheme "-ed" in its written form, pronounced three different ways). Students have reached the stage where they are actually starting to get the morpheme correct some of the time. If you follow one student's pattern of errors in regular past tense across a variety of natural activities in use of oral and written English, you will see that it is an "up and down" process with mastery not occurring instantly once it has been taught or picked up. Instead, gradually over time the student begins to get the morpheme right in more and more contexts until finally the subtleties of the use of that particular structure (e.g. exceptions, spelling variations, pronunciation contexts) has become a subconscious part of the learner's language system. But this takes time, and *formal teaching does not speed up the developmental process.*

Let's take another example: acquisition of the third person singular present tense, which is that simple "-s" added to verbs. ESL textbooks typically introduce this morpheme in beginning lessons. It is easy to teach, because there are few exceptions to the rules for its use. Students may get it right on a written test when they have plenty of time to think about the rule. But most first and second year ESL students will continue to leave off the "-s" when they are speaking or writing English at normal speed. This morpheme does not become a part of the subconscious, acquired system until after several years of exposure to standard English. Many regional varieties of English omit this morpheme in spoken English, so students may hear it less in natural conversational usage. It doesn't hurt to teach the "-s" early, but teachers should not expect students to demonstrate mastery until they have reached the developmental stage when they are ready to pick up its appropriate usage. Acquisition of any given structure in English does not occur simply by formally teaching that structure, but through exposure to correct use of the structure over time in many different linguistic contexts that are meaningful to the student.

This means that *lockstep, sequenced curricular materials that insist on mastery of each discrete point in language before moving onto the next are a disaster for second language acquisition.* The natural order of second language acquisition is a much stronger force than any textbook writer's or teacher's view of simple to complex and other attempts at "logical" sequencing of language points to be mastered. Basic skills approaches don't work because they are often based on some writer's view of the order in which each discrete point in English should be learned, not the natural order. It is especially a disaster to focus on a basic skills, sequenced curriculum when students are thus held back from cognitively complex work appropriate to their maturity level, or when their performance on a discrete-point language test serves as a gatekeeper for access to more meaningful schoolwork.

Then what is the natural order of ESL acquisition? We are still in the early stages of discovering what it might be. Hundreds of studies have been conducted on the order of English morpheme acquisition, because morphemes are easy to isolate, but there are many other aspects of ESL acquisition as well as other English morphemes yet to be analyzed. Krashen (1977) published a generalizable order of ESL morpheme acquisition that, while controversial, remains convincing evidence of general patterns, confirmed by continuing studies (Larsen-Freeman & Long, 1991, pp. 88-92). In this general order, "-ing," the helping verb "to be," and the plural are acquired early. Next are auxiliaries and articles, followed by the irregular past tense. Morphemes acquired late are the regular past tense, third person singular present tense, and the possessive. But I caution you not to overgeneralize from this natural order. While most groups of students fall into this general pattern, individual students can vary from this order of acquisition. Also a teacher cannot expect a student to master a morpheme in one magical moment. Because it is a gradual process, these morphemes overlap, with students reaching varied stages of acquisition of each one at any given time. Another problem with this list is that there are many other English morphemes not yet analyzed.

As teachers, we do not have time to wait for the thousands of studies that would need to be conducted to discover the natural sequence of acquisition of each aspect of English. However, we can recognize that *second language acquisition is a dynamic, creative, innate process, best developed through contextual, meaningful activities that focus on language use, combined with guidance along the way from the teacher that sometimes involves a focus on language form.* The teacher can be a facilitator of the process. In the early acquisition stages, errors need not be viewed as lack of mastery but as positive steps in the process. The focus for beginning ESL students should be on language use, not on language form. As students move along in their exposure to English, second and third year ESL classes can assist with conscious self-editing and development of refinement of rules of the language.

Even so, many rules of language cannot be taught. The English article is a good example. Native speakers of English struggle with proper usage of the article in academic writing at the university level. One teacher cannot begin to teach all the exceptions and subtleties of use of the article. Instead, it is gradually acquired through many years of contact with and use of the language.

One more example of a natural, predictable stage in the developmental process of child second language acquisition is what some linguists call a "silent period" occurring at the beginning of exposure to the new language. For some children, it only lasts a very short time (as little as a couple of days), while for others the silent period can last for several months. ESL beginners who listen but rarely speak in the new language make just as much, and frequently more, progress in second language development as their more talkative classmates, by the end of the first year of exposure to English (Dulay, Burt & Krashen, 1982; Saville-Troike, 1984; Wong Fillmore & Valadez, 1986). Teachers are generally advised to be aware of this natural stage and not to force beginners to speak if they are not yet ready, by developing systems for nonverbal feedback from students in this early stage. Beginning adolescent and adult students may be more influenced by cultural socialization norms or their own emotional feelings than by a predictable silent period, although they, too, might benefit from an initial focus on intensive listening comprehension in the very beginning weeks of ESL instruction.

The Context of Language Use

If a natural, innate process is going on inside our heads as we pick up a second language, how long does it take? The answer to that question depends on many factors, to be discussed throughout this monograph. The first factor that I will present here is the context of language use. *How we plan to use the second language determines the level of proficiency that we want to reach and the length of time that it will take to reach that level.*

SOCIAL LANGUAGE. Striking up a conversation with Manuel in the school corridor, the principal later comments to the school counselor, "I don't know why the ESL teacher insists that Manuel needs another semester of ESL; he speaks perfectly good English." Often we judge a learner's proficiency in English by social language. It's natural to assume that Manuel's conversational fluency extends to all uses of English. But in fact, conversational ability is only a small portion of the language skills needed to be successful in school.

Social language provides extra help to the second language learner, through nonverbal communication and other contextual clues to meaning. In conversations, nonverbal aspects of language have been estimated to be as much as 70 percent of the total communication process (Condon & Yousef, 1975), making oral language very different from written language. *Social language as I am defining it here also includes the development of basic literacy for use in situations such as shopping, use of transportation, access to health services, writing a letter to a friend, or sending an e-mail message. In social language, meaning is negotiated;* in other words, you help each other along through the feedback that you give to your partner in the communication process.

Cummins (1979, 1981, 1986b, 1989a, 1991) has clarified for educators this distinction between social and academic language (to be defined shortly), basing his theories on the work of many researchers before him. In his analyses of Canadian immigrants' school performance on measures of social and academic language, Cummins (1981) reported that children and adolescents acquiring ESL generally develop substantial proficiency in social English within 2-3 years. In an extensive review of studies of language minority children in the U.S., Wong Fillmore concluded that many children develop the oral system of vocabulary, grammar, phonology, semantics, and pragmatics of their second language for their age level over a 2-3 year period, although "differences of up to five years can be found in the time children take to get a working command of a new language" (1991, p. 61). I would like to emphasize here that this range of 2-5 years to acquire social language cited by Wong Fillmore does not even include mastery of reading and writing—only oral English skills.

Furthermore, social language may not develop well in 2-5 years if the conditions are not present for second language acquisition to take place. The following are critical components of the language learning process:

(1) learners who realize that they need to learn the target language and are motivated to do so; (2) speakers of the target language who know it well enough to provide the learners with access to the language and the help they need for learning it; and (3) a social setting which brings learners and target language speakers into frequent enough contact to make language learning possible.

All three components are necessary. If any of them is dysfunctional, language learning will be difficult, or even impossible. When all three are ideal, language learning is assured. Each of them can vary in a great many ways, however, and some of this variation can critically affect the processes by which language is learned.

(Wong Fillmore, 1991b, pp. 52-53)

This generalization from Wong Fillmore is not just her own opinion. It is the undergirding of a major new theory in second language acquisition that was developed over several years of intensive collaboration with many other researchers. Now, perhaps reflecting on your own experiences with learning another language, you may be saying, "So that's why Madame Leblanc didn't have much success with me."

ACADEMIC LANGUAGE. If *it takes 2-5 years to acquire social language,* how long does it take *to acquire academic language?* The answer is a very long time, *a minimum of 7-10 years when schooled all in second language.* Let's first examine the definition and then discuss reasons for the long time needed. I use the term academic language here to represent all the different uses of language in school. From a linguistic perspective, this includes everything listed in the section several pages back on first language acquisition—the phonology, vocabulary, grammar, semantics, pragmatics, and discourse (formal thought patterns) of English across all four language skills—listening, speaking, reading, and writing—increasing in cognitive complexity across each subject area with each succeeding grade level. Academic language is intertwined with cognitive development; they work together. Developing proficiency in academic language thus means catching up and keeping up with native speakers, for eventual successful academic performance at secondary and university levels of instruction—a monumental achievement (Collier & Thomas, 1989).

Academic language is also an extension of social language development. These two dimensions of language are not separate, distinct processes; instead they represent a continuum. Both social and academic language are developed at school. However, academic uses of language become somewhat unique to the school context as students move into increasingly academically demanding work with each succeeding grade level. Each subject—mathematics, science, social studies, language arts—has its own vocabulary, grammar, and discourse patterns unique to that particular field. Linguists call this language register. Each context in which we use language has its own special set of rules for language use. Thus the range of language skills needed expands exponentially at upper grade levels, as students tackle more and more subject areas. Not only is the amount of English expanded, but also subjects are presented mainly through abstract written language with fewer and fewer contextual clues to meaning.

A good teacher includes social and academic language development in every lesson. A class might start with social language development through activities that stimulate students' own knowledge and experience connected to the lesson. As the lesson continues, contextual support can come through peer interaction and use of visuals, maps, charts, manipulatives, the media, technology, music, art, pantomiming.... New knowledge is developed and applied through interactive tasks that stimulate students' cognitive and academic development. Often the first impulse of teachers new to working with ESL students is to water down the curriculum: "They just can't handle it." But they can! Developing ESL academic language means that all students are active participants in classes with meaningful, contextualized language that stimulates their cognitive and academic growth.

How can it take 5-10 years to acquire a second language for schooling purposes? As you can see, it is a complex process. But *the main reason it takes so long is that native speakers are not standing still waiting for ESL students to catch up with them* (Thomas, 1992). Reflecting on the process of first language acquisition that I presented earlier, five-year-olds are not yet halfway through acquiring their first language when they enter school. Their academic language development begins at this age, and two more language skills, reading and writing, are added to their repertoire. Each year they are expanding their vocabulary and developing the special language register of each subject area. Their knowledge base and cognitive development is expanding with each grade level. Cultural knowledge embedded in the native speaker's experiences while growing up adds yet another dimension to the ESL student's language acquisition process.

If you're still skeptical, let's take a look at some of the studies examining academic language development for students schooled in their second language (Collier, 1987, 1989c, 1992c; Collier & Thomas, 1989; Cummins, 1981, 1991, 1992; Cummins & Swain, 1986; Dolson & Mayer, 1992; Genesee, 1987; Ramírez, 1992; Thomas & Collier, 1995). When Cummins (1981) first found that Canadian immigrants were taking 5-7 years to acquire the level of proficiency in English needed to reach age and grade-level norms of native English speakers, U.S. educators expressed surprise that it would take so long. Given the lack of studies examining this important issue, my co-researcher, Wayne Thomas, and I decided to design a series of studies to examine the "how long" question in depth, looking at many factors influencing the process. What we found truly astounded us.

In our first series of studies (Collier, 1987; Collier & Thomas, 1989), we purposely chose a school site where the language minority students were most likely to succeed in a short time—a high-achieving, affluent suburban school district. The sample consisted of over 2,000 immigrant students, 65 percent of whom were Asian in background and 20 percent Hispanic, the rest representing 75 other languages from around the world. These students were from families of middle class or upper middle class background in their home countries. We eliminated from the analyses any immigrant students who entered the school system below grade level in their academic skills. These students received ESL instructional support of 1-3 hours in small classes of 6-12 students, attending mainstream classes the remainder of the day, and were generally exited from ESL within the first two years of their arrival in the U.S.

We found that it took these advantaged and highly motivated immigrant students only two years to surpass the mathematics achievement of native speakers on standardized tests, but it took them 5-10 years to reach native speakers' performance on measures of English reading across the content areas. Those immigrants arriving in the U.S. between the ages of 8-11 made it in 5 years. But younger immigrants arriving at ages 4-7 took 7-10 years to reach the 50th percentile. For these young students, at least two years of schooling in home country turned out to be a very important base for success in second language schooling. The other big surprise of the study was the extremely low achievement of the high school students. They were very well schooled in their home countries and demonstrated that by scoring above the 50th percentile in mathematics in two years after their arrival in the U.S. But after six years of excellent schooling in all English in the U.S., while making steady progress in each subject each year, they had not yet reached the 50th percentile in English language arts, reading, science, and social studies by the time of graduation.

The high cognitive complexity of the material presented at high school and university level demands a much deeper level of language proficiency than that of elementary-school children. But it is not just language development that is the issue. Language is the vehicle for expressing academic and cognitive knowledge. Developing academic language means developing all the academic skills expected of each age level. While ESL adolescents are picking up sufficient beginning-level skills in a second language to be able to follow some of the academic work in their classes, it is inevitable that they are going to fall behind. If it takes a minimum of 2-3 years to acquire social language, then students miss at least that many years of schooling while they are learning basic English. Students in the upper elementary grades have time to catch up. Secondary students are more vulnerable. They miss complex, sequential academic work that is not easily made up. This is one of the reasons for the strong recommendations from researchers to teach ESL through content, so that less time is wasted. The students in our first studies had received traditional ESL instruction, focused exclusively on language development. Subsequent studies that we have conducted have found high school students making faster progress in programs that teach ESL through content areas (Thomas, 1992; Thomas & Collier, 1995).

The problem with getting so far behind in schoolwork is also a rationale for teaching students academic content through their first language. The youngest elementary school students in our studies suffered from not having developed basic literacy in first language; this slowed down their development of literacy in second language. We will examine this issue further in the next section on the role of native language in second language acquisition.

I present our findings in these initial "how long" studies in such detail because we have now replicated the findings in studies in different settings, as have other researchers in additional studies in the U.S. and other countries. Our initial study found that one group made it in four years, but succeeding analyses revealed that it took a minimum of five years for all other groups, and no other researcher has uncovered data that demonstrate reaching norms on standardized tests in less than five years, when students are schooled all in second language.

Then what are the results of students who are schooled bilingually? The answer is that it still takes a long time to demonstrate proficiency in second language comparable to a native speaker. The difference in student performance in a bilingual program, in contrast to an all-English program, is that students typically score at or above grade level in native language in all subject areas, while they are working on learning the second language through academic work. In other words, they do not fall behind in cognitive and academic growth. *After 4-7 years in a quality bilingual program, students typically reach and surpass native speakers' norms in the second language across all subject areas. Furthermore, bilingually schooled students typically sustain this achievement and outperform monolingually schooled students in the upper grades* (Collier, 1992c).

What is intriguing about these findings is that they apply to all students, minority and majority. In Canada, English-speaking students who receive all their schooling bilingually, starting in kindergarten, typically begin to reach native-speaker norms on academic tests given in their second language (French) around fifth or sixth grade (California Department of Education, 1984; Collier, 1992a; Cummins & Swain, 1986; Genesee, 1987; Harley, Allen, Cummins & Swain, 1990; Swain & Lapkin, 1981). Many of these students have every advantage you could ask for, such as highly motivated parents who provide educational support at home, a first language that is not threatened by the broader society, and jobs waiting for them where their bilingual skills are needed, to add to student motivation and expectations. The bottom line is that academic second language proficiency takes a minimum of 4-7 years to develop, no matter how advantaged the circumstances. We are fooling ourselves if we think we can somehow speed up the process.

What we can do, though, is to make sure that we don't slow the process down. The type of instructional support that we give and the sociocultural context established at school have a lot of influence on acquisition of academic second language. In the next section, we will examine the natural, innate linguistic processes that occur in the relationship between a student's first and second languages. Given the supporting role that first language plays in second language acquisition, school decisions regarding this variable should be taken quite seriously and less emotionally.

ROLE OF FIRST LANGUAGE

In the U.S., probably the most sensitive issue in our field that stirs up intense emotional and political debates is the use of public funds to support academic instruction in languages other than English. Foreign language classes for English speakers are widely accepted, but first language instruction for language minority students is considered by many to be a misuse of public funds for schools. This public perception has been fed by media reports that too often present individuals' personal opinions based on no knowledge of the research base. Often recent media reports have given the impression that very few studies have been conducted in our field. Indeed, when bilingual education was expanded in the U.S. in the 1960s, we had a very meager research base explaining the role of the first language. But now, three decades later, we have hundreds of high quality studies that have examined first language development and its relationship to second language and schooling. What do these studies tell us?

ACADEMIC DEVELOPMENT IN FIRST LANGUAGE. *Many, many studies have found that cognitive and academic development in first language has an extremely important and positive effect on second language schooling* (Collier, 1989c, 1992c; Cummins, 1991; Díaz & Klingler, 1991; Freeman & Freeman, 1992; E.García, 1993, 1994; Genesee, 1987, 1994; Hakuta, 1986; Lessow-Hurley, 1990; Lindholm, 1991; McLaughlin, 1992; Snow, 1990; Tinajero & Ada, 1993; Wong Fillmore & Valadez, 1986). Academic skills, literacy development, concept formation, subject knowledge, and learning strategies developed in first language will all transfer to second language. As our ESL students expand their vocabulary and communicative skills in English, they can demonstrate their knowledge base developed in their first language.

For example, in a study that Wayne Thomas and I conducted examining ESL students' mathematics achievement (Collier & Thomas, 1989), 700 adolescent Asian immigrants outperformed native English speakers on a standardized mathematics test administered in English, after only two years of exposure to English in the U.S. These students had received higher levels of mathematics instruction in their home countries before emigrating to the U.S., far ahead of that required in the U.S. curriculum for their grade level. Once they built enough of a base in English mathematics vocabulary, they were able to demonstrate their high level of mathematics knowledge, even though they had not yet taken these courses in English.

Some school districts, frustrated with barriers to ESL students' graduation, have experimented with courses taught in languages other than English. For example, immigrants arriving in the U.S. at high school age, including those on grade level, do not have enough time to acquire the English needed to pass U.S. Government, often a requirement for graduation. By teaching this course in, for example, Vietnamese or Spanish, ESL students have been able to tackle cognitively complex material and demonstrate their mastery of the material, on a test administered in English, in time to graduate. The academic skills and content knowledge transfer from first to second language.

LITERACY IN FIRST LANGUAGE. Let's take a look at transfer of literacy skills, an essential base for all academic work. *Skills developed in first language literacy not only are easily transferred but also are crucial to academic success in the second language* (Au, 1993; Bialystok, 1991; Cummins, 1989a, 1989b, 1991; Cummins & Swain, 1986; Freeman & Freeman, 1992; Genesee, 1987, 1994; Hudelson, 1994; Johnson & Roen, 1989; Lessow-Hurley, 1990; Lindholm, 1991; Snow, 1990; Tinajero & Ada, 1993; Wong Fillmore & Valadez, 1986). *Furthermore, some studies indicate that if students do not reach a certain threshold in first language, including literacy, they may experience cognitive difficulties in second language* (Collier, 1987; Collier & Thomas, 1989; Cummins, 1976, 1981, 1991; Dulay & Burt, 1980; Duncan & De Avila, 1979; Skutnabb-Kangas, 1981). While it is difficult to pinpoint a specific number of years of schooling required for the "threshold" (Cummins, 1976) to be reached, because of great individual variation in second language acquisition, studies that Wayne Thomas and I have conducted have found that students with less than 3-4 years of first language schooling are typically 2 or 3 years behind their

ESL peers in academic achievement in second language (Collier, 1987, 1992c; Collier & Thomas, 1988, 1989).

Surely, you say, not all languages can assist in the acquisition of English literacy. How about non-Roman-alphabet languages such as Arabic, Hindi, Mandarin Chinese, Russian, Hebrew, Korean? Some of these written scripts have right-left or vertical directionality and very different ways of writing phonemes or word symbols. Even so, researchers have found that more than half of the skills acquired in the process of learning to read are universal skills, regardless of the written language system (Chu, 1981; Cummins, 1991; Thonis, 1981). For example, once a student has picked up the significance of following a consistent pattern in directionality, that student has mastered at least half of the skill. Very quickly, a reader of right-left script catches on that English goes left-right and then top to bottom. Having acquired directionality in first language, the student is looking for the pattern of directionality in second language.

Researchers in Canada were surprised to find that first language literacy also has a strong, positive impact on academic achievement in third language, for language minority students attending Canadian bilingual immersion programs taught in French and English. Students' literacy level in their first language was in fact the strongest predictor of academic success in third language (Swain, Lapkin, Rowen & Hart, 1990).

RESEARCH BASE ON THE POSITIVE ROLE OF FIRST LANGUAGE. Cummins (1979, 1981, 1986b, 1991) explains the phenomenon of language transfer as an "interdependence" or "common underlying proficiency" of languages. Universal grammar theories support Cummins's theoretical concept. Research in linguistic universals has found many properties in common across all languages at deep, underlying structural levels (Ellis, 1985). Only in surface structure do languages appear to be radically different.

So, where did the idea come from that is commonly heard among teachers that first language "interferes" with second language? Those of us who have been foreign language teachers watch students making the same mistakes over and over again and on the surface, these errors appear to be "caused" by their first language. But linguists and educators have found that the research evidence strongly implies a positive, supportive role of the first language in second language development, rather than a negative role (Larsen-Freeman & Long, 1991, p. 96). In the early stages of second language acquisition, English learners rely on their experience in their first language as a reference point, a source of knowledge. Subconsciously and sometimes consciously an ESL student will apply structures and patterns from first language to the new language. Through a process of creative construction that involves both listening to and reading English and reflecting on patterns in first language, the English learner gradually catches on to the different patterns of the new language.

But that reliance on first language is now seen by linguists as something very important to the whole process of second language acquisition (Larsen-Freeman & Long, 1991; McLaughlin, 1984, 1985, 1992). The student relies less and less on first language structures as he or she progresses to more advanced stages. In advanced stages of ESL acquisition, studies have found that first language is less an influence in second language vocabulary and grammar development, while first language influence on ESL pronunciation can remain for a lifetime for those beginning exposure to second language as adolescents or adults, what we commonly call an "accent." Retaining some accent in second language is not considered by linguists to be a lack of proficiency, because it is so universal among adolescent and adult learners of a second language.

Another aspect of second language development with fairly strong first language influence at advanced stages of proficiency is formal writing, especially academic writing (Connor & Kaplan, 1987). Thought patterns presented in writing often have hidden cultural values and many other complex aspects of language development, the subtleties of which may never fully be mastered by the adult second language learner. University professors often complain that native English speakers do not reach the higher levels expected in critical analysis and synthesis required of English academic writing. Whether English is our first or second language, throughout our lifetime we continue to acquire new writing skills; it is an endless process.

COGNITIVE DEVELOPMENT IN FIRST LANGUAGE. A commonly held belief in the U.S. is that it is better to "immerse" students in English so that they get maximum exposure to the new language. But more English is not necessarily better. In fact, depending on the circumstances, it may actually slow down students' progress in English. How can that be? *The key to understanding the role of first language in the academic development of second language is to understand the function of uninterrupted cognitive development.*

For communication and cognitive processes, beginning a new language is similar to starting life all over again. As quickly as possible the ESL learner applies all of his/her cognitive knowledge and maturity to the new language. But even in an English-speaking country with maximum exposure to English under ideal conditions for language learning (as opposed to a foreign language context, with very limited exposure to the new language), it takes several years to acquire the surface structure of the language. Earlier we examined the research on acquisition of social language and found that the shortest time was two years, with some children taking up to five years to master the oral system of English. During this period of the first 2 or 3 years of second language acquisition, students may be functioning cognitively at their age level in their first language. But cognitive development in second language is slowed down considerably until they begin to make the leaps needed in acquisition of vocabulary and structures of English to continue higher order thinking at the level of their ability in their first language.

To conceptualize this aspect of language development, imagine yourself as a new learner of Korean. You have been assigned by your company to develop a market for your company's products in Korea, and you have to have some minimal level of competence in Korean to achieve your company's goals. You have made astounding progress in a short time, but over and over again you get frustrated by your lack of vocabulary and fluency in the language to get across the most basic ideas in Korean. It feels like you are a child again. You cannot express the cognitively complex ideas that come so easily in English. In speaking or writing Korean, you are functioning cognitively in Korean at a maturity level far below your age, although you may understand and read Korean at a reasonable level of proficiency.

While as an adult, you may be extremely frustrated in your attempts to use the new language for cognitively complex purposes, at least you have reached cognitive maturity in first language. If you continue your acquisition of Korean, you will eventually be able to apply your cognitive maturity to your second language. But the child being schooled in second language is still going through extensive cognitive development, with dramatic expansion of cognitive processes expected with each succeeding year of schooling. How, then, can we provide for uninterrupted cognitive development for children who are schooled in their second language?

USE OF FIRST LANGUAGE AT HOME. First, we must encourage language minority parents to speak the first language at home, not to speak English. Unfortunately, many, many well-meaning U.S. teachers do just the opposite. The worst advice you can give parents is to speak only English at home. Often language minority parents are not the best source of input for English, but this is not the main reason to discourage the use of English at home. *When parents and children speak the language that they know best, they are working at their level of cognitive maturity. Practicing English at home can actually slow down students' cognitive development.* Well-educated language minority parents can provide crucial first language cognitive support at home and build children's academic knowledge in first language, all of which will transfer to second language being developed at school. Parents who are not formally educated can also provide first language oral development through natural family interaction at home to stimulate the continuation of their children's cognitive processes. For example, cognitive development can happen at home through asking questions, solving problems together, discovering new things, building or fixing something, going somewhere together, cooking food, talking about a TV program, playing music; in other words, experiencing life. Language minority parents, especially those who are recent immigrants, often believe that they should speak English at home and feel guilty when they are not able to speak English comfortably. Once parents understand the importance of cognitive development in first language, they are usually overjoyed to realize that the language that they know best will further their children's growth (Arnberg, 1987; Caplan, Choy & Whitmore, 1992; Collier, 1981, 1986; Delgado-Gaitán, 1990; Dolson, 1985; Genesee, 1994; Moll, Vélez-Ibáñez, Greenberg & Rivera, 1990; Saunders, 1988; Skutnabb-Kangas & Cummins, 1988; Wong Fillmore, 1991a).

USE OF FIRST LANGUAGE AT SCHOOL. Several decades ago in the U.S., it was possible to succeed in life without formal schooling. Most of the stories that you hear about Uncle George's success when he emigrated to the U.S. without any special help are based on experiences of those in the first half of the 20th century. As more professions require formal schooling as a prerequisite to entry into the workforce, we can no longer afford the lost time of 2-3 years (or more) in cognitive and academic development while students are acquiring the surface structure of English. *During the initial years of exposure to English, continuing cognitive and academic development in first language is considered to be a key variable for academic success in second language* (Baker, 1988; Bialystok, 1991; Collier, 1989c, 1992c; Cummins & Swain, 1986; Dolson, 1985; E.García, 1993, 1994; Genesee, 1987, 1994; Hakuta, 1986; Lessow-Hurley, 1990; Snow, 1990; Tinajero & Ada, 1993).

One obvious means of first language support is through formal instruction in a bilingual program. There are many types of bilingual instruction, and these will be discussed in more detail in the section on cognitive processes. We have already examined some of the research on academic language development in a bilingual program. While it takes 4-7 years to develop academic proficiency in second language in a bilingual program, the same amount of time as that required for students receiving only ESL support in the U.S. who have been schooled in home country for at least three years, students schooled bilingually after arrival in the U.S. still have a big advantage over students schooled monolingually in English after arrival. The bilingually schooled students do not fall behind in grade level skills and academic knowledge while they are learning English. When they reach secondary level, the bilingually schooled students are able to maintain their academic gains, even though they might be schooled only in English in high school. In contrast, the monolingually schooled students, who appeared to be doing well in elementary school, typically are not able to sustain their achievement levels and drop substantially in academic achievement at secondary school level. Furthermore, when I have examined patterns of long-term achievement of language minority students who enter U.S. schools below grade level in their academic work, these students can much more efficiently catch up and keep up by receiving intense academic instruction in their first language, all of which will eventually transfer to second language.

Here is another example of the positive role first language schooling can play. The state of California decided a few years ago to try an experiment with preschool Spanish-speaking children. Families with the lowest income levels were invited to enroll their children in 23 Montessori preschools in which the language of instruction was exclusively Spanish. As the graduates of these preschools have entered public elementary schools, they are so far ahead in academic skills and self-confidence that they have outperformed their peers in every academic content area, even though they are not introduced to the English language until first or second grade (Spiegel-Coleman, Wong Fillmore, personal communication).

Even given the strong successes that quality bilingual programs have had in the academic achievement of language minority students, school systems in the U.S. do not yet have the resources needed to provide first language instruction for all language groups. Given this practical reality, there are still many ways that educators can provide a supportive environment for first language development. Here are some suggestions:
- Teaching some academic content courses in first language
- Hiring bilingual school staff (including the librarian, janitor, counselor...)

- Using volunteer tutors who are proficient in students' first languages (including parents, cross-age, and peer tutors)
- Providing books, dictionaries, and other resources in students' first languages in the library and all classrooms
- Preparing units in lessons that incorporate other languages in a meaningful way (such as bilingual storytellers, first language pen pals across classes or schools through e-mail, journal writing in first language, environmental print in first language for young readers, show and tell in first language, learning centers in first language)
- Building partnerships with parents to continue first language cognitive and academic development at home
- Using the school building for after-school or weekend school taught in students' first language(s)
- Encouraging students to contribute articles in first language to student publications
- Inviting ethnic community members as resource persons
- Allowing social use of first language outside of classes
- Encouraging extracurricular activities and school celebrations in students' first languages
- Providing signs throughout the school in the different languages of the community
- Sending newsletters and school information to parents in first language
- Providing family math and literacy programs in evenings or weekends.
  (Collier, 1981, 1986; Cummins, 1989a; Freeman & Freeman, 1992; Ovando & Collier, 1995; Scarcella, 1990; Tinajero & Ada, 1993.)

Once educators and parents can realize that students are losing at least 2 or 3 years of schooling while they are acquiring a basic knowledge of English, the reasons for development of academic skills in first language become more apparent. *Whatever cognitive and academic support in first language can be provided, through higher education courses, adult education literacy programs, bilingual education in public schools, after-school or weekend community schools, and parents' support for first language cognitive development at home, will benefit students' academic achievement in second language.* Language minority parents who have not had any past opportunity to attend formal schooling can also benefit from after-school and weekend support programs that build family literacy and mathematics skills in first language (Collier, 1986; Delgado-Gait†n, 1990). Creating a school and higher education environment that recognizes the importance of first language in people's lives is crucial for second language academic success.

AGE DIFFERENCES

Often I am asked, "What is the ideal age to begin a second language?" As usual, there is no easy answer. Your age can make a difference when you first begin learning a second language. But to understand how age affects the acquisition process, you need to consider many other variables that interact with age. Age does not operate in isolation as a cause agent. Since we teachers have no way to change the ages of our students, it is important to know that students of all ages can be very effective learners of language. At the same time, each age group can experience different interacting factors that influence the acquisition process. Let's take a look at general patterns in age differences.

INFANTS AND TODDLERS: SIMULTANEOUS BILINGUALS. Young children who are raised from birth with exposure to two languages experience a process similar to first language acquisition. Using their innate language capacity, most children go through an initial stage of combining the two languages into one system. As they move through succeeding stages, assuming that they receive approximately equal exposure to the two languages, they gradually learn to separate the two languages into two distinct systems by around age five or six.

For young bilinguals, *language mixing during the preschool years is quite common as a natural stage in the developmental process of language acquisition. It is a big mistake to diag-*

nose language mixing as a learning disability for this age group. As long as a young child receives regular exposure to both languages over time, and experiences continuing cognitive development in both languages, he or she will reach the same level of proficiency in two languages as that of a child acquiring one language (Goodz, 1994; Hakuta, 1986; Harding & Riley, 1986; Hatch, 1978; McLaughlin, 1984). Furthermore, children who are fortunate enough in school to be able to continue building academic proficiency in both languages are likely to experience cognitive advantages over monolinguals (Baker, 1993; Bialystok, 1991; Díaz & Klingler, 1991; Genesee, 1987; Hakuta, 1986).

Parents often worry that they should separate the two languages, with, for example, one parent speaking only Spanish and the other speaking only English. This used to be the advice given to parents several decades ago. But we now have considerable research evidence that separating the two languages is not necessary, as long as both languages are used on a relatively equal basis by those with whom the child interacts, so that the child gets equal exposure to and practice with the two languages. The child will eventually sort out the two language systems by around school age as part of the natural, subconscious process.

PRESCHOOLERS: SUCCESSIVE BILINGUALS. Children who begin a second language sometime during the preschool years can be equally successful second language learners. However, one major interacting factor is crucial—continuing cognitive development in first language. Often well-meaning educators feel that preschoolers can get a head start on acquiring ESL by immersing the children in English at the expense of their first language. At this stage of their schooling, they usually appear to be doing very well. But those children whose cognitive development in first language was stopped or slowed down in the preschool years tend to perform poorly on school measures across the curriculum as they move into the upper elementary grades. Cummins (1976, 1977) refers to this phenomenon as a "threshold" that must be reached in first language in order to reach high cognitive levels in second language, as discussed in the previous section.

Children of low socioeconomic background or those whose parents have not had the opportunity to receive formal schooling are those most in danger of lost years of cognitive development, due to an early switch to the second language in preschool (Wong Fillmore, 1991a). These children are better prepared academically when they attend preschool that is taught exclusively in their home language. In other words, at this age, cognitive development is much more important than introduction to second language. For these children, exposure to second language should be postponed until a solid cognitive and academic base is built in first language.

The state of California made a decision in the early 1980s to conduct research to examine this phenomenon. They established a number of "Case Study" schools and followed students' progress through elementary schools that teach language minority students through their home language until second or third grade, when English is introduced in the curriculum for the first time. In these schools, first language academic instruction is continued for at least half a day throughout the elementary school grades. Through this program model, the state has greatly improved the academic achievement of language minority students (California Department of Education, 1991; Krashen & Biber, 1988).

AGES 5-11. Continuing cognitive and academic development in first language is also a crucial issue for children in elementary school. Success in second language is more likely if literacy and thinking skills are fully developed in first language through fifth or sixth grade. *This age group (5-11 years) is a great time to begin a second language. In fact, any age from birth to age 12 is a good time as long as cognitive and academic development in first language is not stopped or slowed down* (Bialystok, 1991; Collier, 1988, 1989c, 1992c).

The big advantage children from birth to puberty have over older learners is pronunciation. The younger you are when you begin a second language, the less likely it is that you will retain or even develop an accent. Native-like pronunciation is not really a proficiency issue, assuming that you can be well understood with your accent. However, an accent can often change the social perceptions that native speakers have about you, such as their assuming that you have very limited proficiency in the language, which can be quite frustrating, sometimes resulting in discriminatory treatment. Pronunciation is a concern for adolescents, young adults, and older adults, to be discussed next.

ADOLESCENTS AND YOUNG ADULTS. A research synthesis on the optimal age for beginning second language, written more than ten years ago (Krashen, Scarcella & Long, 1982), concluded that "older is faster but younger is better." Research since that publication has found that this generalization applies mainly to social language development, not to academic language development (Collier, 1988, 1989c). Adolescents and young adults have many advantages over the younger child, if they have received formal schooling in their first language. Young adults' academic knowledge and experience with schooling assist them in second language schooling. *Except for pronunciation, students of this age group are the most efficient learners of a second language, because they are cognitively mature.*

The main reason that we are fooled by young children's ability in second language is that the type of language a five-year-old speaks is much less cognitively complex than that of a young adult. We are also often jealous of the native-like pronunciation that young children acquire quickly and their seeming ease in social interaction with speakers of the second language. But the process young children are going through is just as complex as the experience of older learners, and it takes more time for young children to reach academic proficiency in second language than for high school and university students, who have reached cognitive maturity and can transfer all their academic knowledge base acquired in first language to the second language.

High school students have to worry about not getting behind academically while they are learning the second language. This is even a more urgent issue for older students who have received little or no formal schooling. For these students, the most efficient way of catching up academically is through instruction in first language. Again, *cognitive and academic development is a higher priority than exposure to the second language, for ultimate academic success.*

ADULTS. Adult learners of a second language who are beyond their 20s when first introduced to the new language may have more difficulty than the adolescent or young adult (Harley, 1986; Long, 1988; Scovel, 1988). We have already discussed the issue of pronunciation, which is a concern for adults as well as adolescents and young adults. But older adults are quite capable of developing full proficiency in the second language with time, except for the inevitability of retaining an accent in pronunciation. At the same time, there are "maturational constraints" (Long, 1988) that can influence the process for adults, such as social access to speakers of the second language and a tendency to experience less cognitive flexibility as we get older. Older adults have been quite successful with third and fourth language acquisition if they are already very proficient in their first two languages.

Overall, stating that one age is better than another to begin second language acquisition is misleading. This greatly oversimplifies the complex linguistic, sociocultural, cognitive, and academic factors that interact with age in the development of second language (Collier, 1987, 1988, 1989c, 1992a). The following sections continue our examination of these interacting factors.

INPUT AND INTERACTION

One more aspect essential to the natural linguistic process is the type of input provided to ESL learners. Earlier when we examined social language, I presented the most critical components of language learning: a native English speaker and an English learner working together in a social setting that encourages natural and meaningful interaction (Wong Fillmore, 1991b). To structure the classroom so that this natural interaction takes place, traditional teacher-centered instruction must be rejected as inadequate. Instead, *classes that are highly interactive, emphasizing student problem-solving and discovery learning through thematic experiences across the curriculum are likely to provide the kind of social setting for natural language acquisition to take place.*

The teacher is an important source of input for the students. In a foreign language class, the teacher may be the only model of the new language. But in a second language setting where the new language is the dominant language of the society, peers are the most important source of input to the learner. We may prefer that the ESL student pay more attention to us, but research shows that peers are preferred over adults. Given that reality, structuring our classes so that students naturally interact with each other as they work on acquisition of new knowledge will lead to natural second language acquisition.

What type of input is most helpful? Krashen (1981, 1982, 1985) says that *English that is understood, natural, interesting, useful for meaningful communication, and roughly one step beyond the learner's present level of proficiency is most beneficial.* Linguists have found that we naturally modify our speech without thinking when we speak to someone who does not understand us very well. We do this in "caregiver speech" with a baby or young child, as well as in "foreigner talk" and "teacher talk." Some natural strategies in caregiver speech are to focus on the here and now, shortening sentences, repeating through rephrasing, correcting errors indirectly, inserting pauses, and focusing on communication rather than on correcting grammar forms (Berko Gleason, 1993; de Villiers & de Villiers, 1978; Snow & Ferguson, 1977; Wells, 1985). With ESL students, teachers use nonverbal pauses, gestures, and facial expressions; a great variety of visual aids and manipulatives; changes in volume and manner of delivery; repetitions, paraphrases, and expansions; comprehension checks; and simplification of grammar patterns (Smallwood, 1992). To provide the best input, linguists recommend just being natural, not distorting pronunciation or exaggerating features of English, but speaking with natural conversational style as though talking to a native speaker.

In addition, written input comes from reading. The most useful texts for second language learners have the same characteristics as input for spoken language. Meaningful readings are written in readable, natural language that is interesting, useful, and roughly one step beyond the learner's present level of proficiency in English (Krashen, 1985). Also readings are meaningful when they are cognitively appropriate for a student's maturity level and they connect to a student's past experiences and knowledge base. For example, a text that presents a bicultural or multicultural perspective is crucial to activate students' background knowledge and stimulate the second language acquisition process (Au, 1993; Smallwood, 1991; Tharp & Gallimore, 1988; Tinajero & Ada, 1993).

Output is also essential (Swain, 1985). Output is speaking and writing in the second language. After making it through the initial silent period, the ESL learner needs to have lots of opportunities to speak in English. And from the first day of exposure to English, ESL students can begin the acquisition of reading and writing. Allowing ESL students to engage in extensive interaction with their peers is crucial to their receiving meaningful input, because it is through communication with friends that they can influence the type of language spoken to them so that it actually becomes meaningful. Likewise, writing as experienced through the writing process stimulates feedback from peers and the teacher which then leads to new language acquisition (Enright & McCloskey, 1988; Freeman & Freeman, 1992; Goodman & Wilde, 1992; Hudelson, 1994; Johnson & Roen, 1989). In summary, *oral and written language in which meaning is negotiated between ESL learners and native English speakers is central to the language acquisition process* (Allwright & Bailey, 1991; Chaudron, 1988; Ellis, 1985, 1990; Gass & Madden, 1985; Hatch, 1983; Swain, 1985; Wong Fillmore, 1989, 1991b).

Social & Cultural Processes

Now that we have examined some of the natural, subconscious linguistic processes that occur inside the learner's head, let's take a look at another major aspect of second language acquisition: the sociocultural dimension. **Social and cultural processes have a powerful influence on language development in an education context.** I am referring to factors such as past experiences students have had that continue to affect their present lives, such as escape from war or from an economically depressed country, amount of past schooling, or socioeconomic status, past and present. This dimension also includes the school environment in which students are schooled, such as a cooperative or competitive learning environment, school attitudes toward affirmation or denigration of students' first languages and cultural backgrounds, as well as teachers valuing the affective or emotional side of learning. Other examples include societal factors, such as social and psychological distance between first and second language speakers, perceptions of each group in interethnic relations, cultural stereotyping, intergroup hostility, subordinate status of a minority group in a given region, and patterns of assimilation (losing first culture when acquiring second culture) or acculturation (acquiring and affirming both first and second cultures).

Interrelationships among Sociocultural, Linguistic, Cognitive, and Academic Dimensions of Language Acquisition

To understand the relationship between this sociocultural dimension of language acquisition and the linguistic and cognitive dimensions, I have created a figure that symbolizes the overall process of language acquisition. While this figure looks two-dimensional on paper, you can use your imagination to picture it as a prism with multiple dimensions.

FIGURE 1
Language Acquisition for School

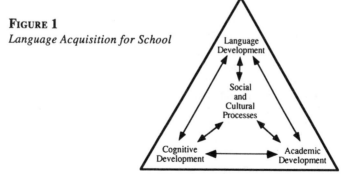

At the heart of the figure is the individual student, influenced by the social and cultural processes surrounding that student in everyday life with family and community and expanding to school, the region, and society—in the past, present, and future. These social and cultural processes have influence on all three domains of development—cognitive, academic, and language processes. *The four dimensions presented in the figure are interdependent. If one is developed to the neglect of another, this may be detrimental to a student's overall growth and future success.*

We have seen in the first section of this monograph that the natural, subconscious aspects of language development are a resource, or an innate ability present in all humans. With appropriate teaching strategies in a school context that is socioculturally supportive of students with diverse needs, the magic can happen in language acquisition. But *language acquisition is not one-dimensional. Both first and second languages need to be developed to a deep level of proficiency, for maximum cognitive growth. Likewise, a program that emphasizes only English language development may neglect academic and cognitive development, which are equally important for future academic success and functioning in English.* Thus the three developmental dimensions of language acquisition for school—linguistic, cognitive, and academic processes—interact with each other and with the sociocultural dimension of learning in complex ways.

As can be seen in Figure 1, *social and cultural factors are at the heart of the process, influencing all aspects of linguistic, cognitive, and academic development.* Language acquisition for school occurs in a social context—the classroom, the school, the community, the region, and the broader society. A student's past and present social contexts have a strong influence on the process of that student's acquisition of second language for school. This dimension of language acquisition may feel very frustrating to conscientious educators because we have little influence on these mostly external factors. Yet, even though we have little chance to change societal patterns, *we can modify the existing social context within schools through changes in instructional practices and administrative structures to provide the most supportive social context for our students' successful acquisition of second language and academic achievement.*

As we visit several examples of sociocultural processes at work in second language acquisition, keep in mind that these are only tiny glimpses of very complex issues. Extensive research from anthropology, sociology, sociolinguistics, and education has been conducted on these powerful sociocultural influences on the acquisition/learning process. This quick review just barely skims the surface.

Escape from War or from an Economically Depressed Region

Immigrants who are recent arrivals to the United States come from all regions of the world. Major political upheavals and instant worldwide communications are producing global mobility at a rate never before seen on this planet. In the 1990s, the changes occurring in eastern Europe and the former Soviet Union, movement toward democratic forms of government in many other regions of the world, and more worldwide awareness of the economic contrasts in quality of life from one region to another, have led to major movement of peoples around the world. The U.S. is only one of many nations in all parts of the world that are currently experiencing a dramatic increase in the flow of immigrants arriving daily (Sharry, 1994; Stewart, 1993).

Among our new arrivals are many undocumented as well as legal refugees seeking refuge from war or from severe economic conditions or from political oppression. These students bring to our classes special social, emotional, and academic needs. They are risk-takers with human potential who hope for a better life (Jamieson & Seaman, 1993). At the same time, they may have experienced interrupted schooling in their home countries, such as fewer school hours per day because of overcrowded schools, or limited accessibility to formal schooling in remote or rural regions, or missed years of schooling because of war or political instability. Those who are fleeing from war may have been through devastating personal experiences, such as family members murdered or lost, emotionally scarring brutality and violence, years spent in crowded refugee camps, or other possible horrors. Students escaping war often exhibit symptoms of post-traumatic stress disorder, such as depression, withdrawal, hyperactivity, aggression, and intense anxiety in response to situations that recall traumatic events in their lives (Coelho, 1994, p. 313).

Often younger immigrants to the U.S. do not come of their own will. They may be encouraged to flee being drafted into the military in their home countries, or they may be sent unaccompanied by parents to escape escalating violence, or they may join family members in the U.S. who are strangers to them as they attempt to lead new lives. They are often frightened, angry, bitter, but may also be hopeful and energized in their new country. Bilingual counselors can provide important emotional support as they attempt to sort out their lives.

Very little research has been conducted on *recent arrivals who have been through traumatic experiences and have little or no formal first language schooling.* These students *especially need lots of first language academic support, to develop literacy, mathematics, science, and social studies knowledge as efficiently as possible to make up missed years of academic instruction.* In special bilingual and ESL programs developed for students from war-torn areas, *some students also need lots of emotional support and counseling to deal with the scars of violence they have witnessed, and the continuing trauma of establishing stable family relations in their new country and meeting their basic survival needs.*

Trueba, Jacobs and Kirton (1990) provide an analysis of one Indochinese refugee group's adaptation to life in the United States—Hmong children who escaped war and emigrated from refugee camps to central California. After describing these Hmong students' adaptation process, the researchers concluded that bicultural learning environments were needed "to break the vicious cycle of stress, poor performance, humiliation, depression and failure" experienced in U.S. schools by many immigrant groups with traumatic past experiences (p. 109). The researchers recommend bicultural school activities that integrate first language, culture, and community knowledge, so that each academic task is meaningfully connected to students' prior knowledge. In Hawaii, Arizona, and California, language minority students of several different cultural heritages and past educational and emotional experiences have been able to increase their academic achievement significantly through bicultural learning environments (Tharp & Gallimore, 1988).

Another study of Indochinese refugees examined 6,750 Southeast Asian boat people who emigrated to the U.S. following devastating hardships suffered in war and relocation camps (Caplan, Choy & Whitmore, 1992). The researchers collected extensive data from Indochinese families living in the U.S., including interviews conducted in first language and students' grade point averages and standardized test scores. Contrary to the researchers' expectations, they found that the strongest predictors of these Indochinese students' academic success in U.S. schools were parents' maintenance of first language at home through conversation and reading books in first language together, as well as an emphasis on strong retention of their own cultural traditions and values, including providing a supportive home environment for valuing education. The families in the study were found not to have had extensive opportunities for formal schooling in the past in their home countries, due to education having been a privilege mainly for the upper classes. Yet in spite of parents' lack of formal education, they were able to provide the family support needed for their children to do academically well in second language, through maintenance and continuing development of first language and cultural heritage at home.

Influence from Other Student Variables

Often teachers assume that the language a student speaks or the country a student comes from might be a strong predictor variable influencing eventual success in second language. However, no particular first language or specific home country, by itself, is a significant influence on academic achievement in second language. This myth has been disproven in many methodologically well conducted studies. In other words, students of all language backgrounds have equal ability to reach proficiency in ESL for schooling. *Individual variation will produce differences in the rate of acquisition of second language among students due to social and affective factors, but not due to the specific first language a student speaks or the particular home country the student comes from.*

The most powerful variable, instead, is the amount of quality formal schooling the student has experienced in first language. The more cognitive and academic development a student has had in first language, the better he or she will be able to achieve academically in second language (Collier, 1989c, 1992c). Differences that ESL teachers observe among students of different language backgrounds are short-term differences in the first years of exposure to English. In the early stages of language learning, students rely heavily on first language structures to figure out their second language, and teachers can more visibly see first language transfer. But this is a short-term phenomenon and not a long-term predictor of differences in success in second language.

Likewise, home country by itself is not a predictor. Instead, the particular social circumstances surrounding a student's past experiences—such as war, or severe poverty, or lack of schooling—are the more powerful influences on success in second language for schooling. And yet, while these can be very powerful variables, they do not necessarily predict failure in second language schooling. A school environment that recognizes what students have been through and provides the social, emotional, and academic support can successfully modify the power of past social circumstances.

Another example is socioeconomic status. In education research of the 1960s and 1970s, socioeconomic status (SES) was identified as one of the most powerful variables influencing student achievement in schools. Students of low SES were identified and given individualized instruction in language arts and mathematics. A common approach to language teaching was to assume that students of low SES background were best taught through a carefully structured, sequenced, basic skills approach. After two decades of research, educators have found that simplified texts and discrete-skills teaching isolated from meaningful contexts actually widens the gap in achievement between middle-class and low-SES students as they move into cognitively and academically more complex material with each succeeding grade level. Whole language approaches to language teaching are now embraced by researchers in language arts, because of their closer match with the natural language acquisition process, and most of all, because of the potential these approaches have for closing the gap in academic achievement among students of varied income backgrounds (as well as of culturally and linguistically diverse backgrounds). Research shows that changes in instructional practices can lessen the power of the background variable of socioeconomic status (National Coalition of Advocates for Students, 1988; Oakes, 1985, 1992; Rothman, 1991; Valdez Pierce, 1991).

For language minorities, severe poverty is not necessarily closely correlated with second language academic failure. Past and present circumstances for each culturally and linguistically diverse person and family in the U.S. vary greatly. For example, most new immigrants in the U.S. have been through some kind of shift in SES from home country to host country. Some have abandoned a comfortable middle- or upper-class life in their home country and must then go through reestablishing themselves professionally in the host country, which often involves at least a temporary shift to lower income levels. Others experience upward mobility within a short time after emigration. Still others in urban areas may remain in the same type of poverty that they left in their home country, with little hope for a better life. SES variations among language minority students do not strongly influence students' academic achievement in second language, in the same way that SES influences native speaker achievement. For example, among some immigrants, the desire for education as one key to upward mobility has provided the fuel to overcome SES as a powerful variable. Recent research on effective schools for language minority students has found that low SES is a less powerful variable for students in schools that provide a strong bilingual/bicultural, academically rich context for instruction (Collier, 1992c; Cummins, 1989a; Krashen & Biber, 1988; Lucas, Henze & Donato, 1990; Rothman, 1991; Valdez Pierce, 1991).

Societal Factors in the United States

Now that we have taken a brief look at some external social factors that students bring to the classroom from their past experiences, let's examine a few examples of the broader social context in which our students are schooled. Within the social context for a given community or region, there are many potential sociocultural influences on the acquisition of second language for schooling. These are often strong, powerful influences. They can be most frustrating for school staff because we sometimes feel powerless to change or modify these circumstances. Yet by creating a school culture different from the society surrounding the school, staff and students together can recreate and shape the sociocultural context for schooling.

Societal factors that influence schooling usually revolve around relations between groups. Earlier we listed some of these types of factors, *such as social and psychological distance created between first and second language speakers, perceptions of each group in interethnic comparisons, cultural stereotyping, intergroup hostility, or subordinate status of a minority group* (Brown, 1994; McLaughlin, 1985; Schumann, 1978). For example, new ESL learners can become quite isolated from peer native-speaker models of English, depending on the social circumstances. *To activate the natural second language acquisition process, ESL learners do not need 16 hours of exposure to English per day. But they do need around 2-3 hours per day of quality interaction with native speakers during which time they are respected as equal partners in school.* This seems easy but it often does not happen naturally, especially for young adolescents in middle school and adolescents in high school. There are many ways in which social and psychological barriers, sometimes created in very subtle ways, and other times presented as open disrespect, can limit our ESL learners' access to natural English input from peers. For ESL adult learners, often the social distance from native speakers is created through social barriers in the professional hierarchy.

Majority-minority and inter-ethnic relations, as well as social class differences, are at the heart of these factors influencing second language acquisition and success in school. One pattern which is very real and difficult to change is the human tendency to create social hierarchies, based on perceptions (usually misperceptions) of groups. For example, a common pattern in majority-minority relations is subconsciously to relegate one or more minority groups in a given region to subordinate status. Members of that group might experience discrimination in many subtle and blatant ways, might be denied jobs and housing, and might as a group do extremely poorly in school.

Among the more insightful but depressing analyses of this pattern in the U.S. are studies by John Ogbu, a Nigerian-American anthropologist at the University of California at Berkeley. Ogbu (1974, 1978, 1987, 1992, 1993) concludes that the U.S. is essentially a caste society, excluding true participation of subordinate minority groups in access to education or career opportunities for advancement. He defines subordinate minorities as indigenous groups who were brought by force to the U.S. or whose land was taken over by the U.S. Cummins (1986a, 1989a) and others have challenged U.S. schools to break this hierarchical societal pattern by creating school communities that radically change majority-minority relations. For example, two-way developmental bilingual education helps to equalize relations between language majority and language minority speakers. (We will examine this program model in the last section of this monograph on cognitive and academic development.)

Other researchers have found many patterns of differential treatment for minority groups in schools that may lead to denial of access to education services. Oakes (1985, 1992) has found extensive evidence of institutionalized racial bias in the U.S. education system, with minority students still being counseled into non-academic tracks and generally denied many educational opportunities. She strongly advocates major U.S. education reform to eliminate tracking and ability grouping. Minicucci and Olsen (1992) have found that even when school staff work hard to set up what they feel are more appropriate and meaningful curricula for language minority students at secondary level, the establishment of special classes (in this case, sheltered content classes) can lead to denial of access to courses needed to graduate or to pursue higher education. Suárez-Orozco (1987, 1993) has examined inequality and discrimination in U.S. schools through the experiences of Central American immigrants. Eisenhart & Graue (1993) point out that group boundaries can be redefined in school. In other words, as students interact in schools, societal group patterns do not necessarily dictate the way that students will ultimately choose to define their group memberships. School structures such as ability grouping and tracking can create unfortunate social distance between groups. On the other hand, *school practices that encourage inclusion and positive perceptions of school have real potential to break societal social and cultural patterns.*

Another example of studies examining school inequities focuses on the role of one program model, transitional bilingual education, in the segregation of language minority students and thus subconsciously maintaining the status quo in majority-minority relations (Hernández-Chávez, 1977, 1984; Spener, 1988). In the 1970s, transitional bilingual programs were originally designed to be short-term, segregated programs for language minority students of one home language background. The negative social perception that both English-speaking and language minority peers developed of these classes in schools too often led to these students' social isolation. Today, we are moving away from thinking of these classes as short-term, remedial solutions. Instead, first-language academic development is encouraged as a long-term process, and English-speaking students who are interested in acquiring another language through meaningful academic content (rather than boring foreign language drills) are encouraged to enroll in the bilingual classes along with their language minority peers. *To break the cycle of bilingual classes being perceived as remedial in nature, they must be a permanent, desired, integral part of the curriculum, taught through quality instruction that encourages interactive, problem-solving, experiential learning.*

Cummins (1986a, 1989a, 1989b) and other authors (Delgado-Gaitán, 1990; Freire & Macedo, 1987; McCaleb, 1994; Skutnabb-Kangas & Cummins, 1988; Shor & Freire, 1987; Tinajero & Ada, 1993) have used the term "empowerment" to symbolize the struggles embodied in each group's access to education and overall success in life. Empowerment includes shared decision-making among parents, teachers, students, and administrators. Delgado-Gaitán (1987, 1990) describes the need for closer school-community relations through analyzing language minority parents' perceptions of school and their role in school decision-making. *In a school with a very heterogeneous population, empowerment implies developing curricula, instructional methods, assessment practices, and administrative structures that provide interdisciplinary, meaningful, high quality academic problem-solving within a multicultural, global perspective.*

The Classroom Environment and Affective Factors

Within the general category of social and cultural processes that influence second language acquisition, another important consideration is the social context within the classroom. *Teachers who recognize the importance of the affective, or emotional, side of learning are crucial for students' long-term growth.* All students bring many different types of learning styles, emotional responses, and personality differences to their everyday work in the classroom. *As we respond to our students, we need to create a supportive classroom environment that values each student and the individual strengths and resources he or she brings to the learning process.* Research in second language acquisition has shown that students with self-confidence, self-esteem, and lowered anxiety are better learners (Brown, 1994; Krashen, 1982; Richard-Amato, 1988; Schumann, 1978). Research on students' learning styles has found that we are as diverse in the ways that we approach learning as we are diverse as a species in our cultural and linguistic heritages (Brown, 1994; Oxford, 1990). Furthermore, we are not stagnant. We constantly change in response to interactions with others. *Therefore, a teacher's best strategy is to use many different instructional approaches to meet the diverse needs of learners.* Conscious development of many types of learning strategies is an important new approach to teaching language minority students that we will explore in the section on cognitive processes (Chamot & O'Malley, 1994; Oxford, 1990).

Another instructional strategy with great promise is the use of cooperative learning as a classroom management structure for grouping students in many different ways to allow for peer interaction and discovery learning (Kagan, 1986, 1992). There are many reasons for using cooperative learning to modify the influence of social and cultural factors in language minority schooling. It provides a manageable structure for cooperative peer interaction, crucial for natural second language acquisition (Faltis, 1993; Wong Fillmore, 1989, 1991b). Cooperative learning also helps develop prosocial skills among sometimes hostile groups and leads to dramatic academic gains, especially for students at risk (Johnson & Johnson, 1986; Kagan, 1986; Slavin, 1988).

Language Use at School

Another seemingly simple issue that is fraught with social, emotional, and cultural complications centers around the practices and policies regarding students' use of their first languages at school. Earlier in this monograph, I discussed the extensive research base supporting the important role that first language plays in academic and cognitive development. But when this issue is discussed rationally, many U.S. educators still respond very emotionally. Public discussions continue to be presented in the national media, as though personal opinions pro and con can decide the issue, and research continues to be ignored. Why do we let our emotions decide this issue? It has to do with the sociocultural complications that surround the decisions regarding language use at school.

In U.S. schools of the 19th century, we were very tolerant regarding the use of multiple languages for instructional and social purposes (Crawford, 1992a; Kloss, 1977). But in the first half of the 20th century, as a nation we worked on forging a national identity at the expense of attempted repression of diversity. During this period, educational historians describe countless examples of repression of minority language use at school, including extensive use of physical punishment (Crawford, 1992a; Tyack, 1974). Now as we approach the end of the 20th century, as a nation we have established an identity, but we are still ambivalent about tolerance of diversity, although we generally admit that our diversity is our strength. Yet we continue to experience a generally intolerant, or ambivalent attitude toward multiple languages (Crawford, 1992a, 1992b).

In most other countries, bilingualism or multilingualism is the norm, across all social classes and all age groups, for everyday life and in many professional settings (O.García, 1991; Grosjean, 1982). In contrast, in the U.S., we have attempted to eradicate bilingualism as quickly as possible, by strong societal pressure on each immigrant group to switch to exclusive use of English, which generally occurs by second or third generation. *We complain that new immigrants are not learning English, but sociolinguists have found that this is just not true. Language shift to monolingualism in English occurs faster in the U.S. than in any other country in the world* (Grosjean, 1982; Veltman, 1988). We get confused by the rapid influx of new immigrants arriving daily, so that many immigrants are at multiple levels of proficiency development in second language, and the layperson's perception is that "they're not learning English."

Yet for some second and third generation immigrants, bilingualism persists, in spite of this strong societal pressure to eradicate immigrants' first languages, because our first language is intimately connected to our personal identity. It is our first means of expression of soul, kinship, emotions, tastes, sounds, and smells. It is our language of intimacy, our close connection to family, the essence of our being. To deny a child the only means of communicating with his parents or to denigrate an adolescent for expressing her emotions through first language is tantamount to physical violence towards that student.

Then *what forces are at work to bring about this societal pressure to lose first language? Majority-minority relations are the heart of the issue.* Patterns of school language use often reflect language status within a given community. *When the majority group wishes to keep a minority group in subordinate status, school rules prohibiting the use of languages other than English are often used to maintain unequal relations between groups, by enforcing use of the majority language for all instructional and social contexts in school. The dominant group thus maintains control.* Use of a minority language at school often is interpreted as a threat or an insult by monolingual majority language speakers. But there are wonderful counterexamples of schools where staff and students affirm and celebrate the use and importance of multiple languages, in both social and instructional contexts.

Lambert (1975, 1984) refers to the phenomenon of heavy societal pressure leading to gradual loss of a minority language as subtractive bilingualism. Subtractive bilingualism occurs as a consequence of social pressure sometimes present in majority-minority relations. *The major danger of subtractive bilingualism is when first language is lost at too young an age, sometimes resulting in negative cognitive effects, as well as lost communication with parents* (Cummins, 1976, 1977, 1979; Wong Fillmore, 1991a). *But even for older students in upper elementary, middle, and secondary schools, subtractive bilinguals (losing first language) perform less well on many cognitive and academic measures than additive bilinguals (acquiring second language while maintaining or expanding proficiency in first language)* (Collier, 1992c).

Schools reflect the community and the broader society. But they do not have to be limited by existing societal patterns. Schools can be agents of change, or places where teachers, students, and staff of many varied backgrounds join together and transform tensions between groups that currently exist. One current movement taking place right now is the growth of two-way developmental bilingual schools, where language-majority parents have joined together with language-minority parents to choose a quality academic curriculum taught through two languages, with the goal of additive bilingualism for all students, majority and minority. With equal status given to the two languages through the instructional program, these programs have achieved the highest success rate in long-term student achievement, for both minority and majority students (Thomas & Collier, 1995). Even in schools with no instructional support for minority languages, staff can modify existing societal patterns (that often lead to low academic achievement of language minority students) by respecting the functions that first language serves for self-identity and cognitive development, as well as social and emotional support. Decisions can be made for social language use as well as counseling and tutoring support in students' first languages that will significantly assist students' affirmation of schools as a place where they want to grow and learn.

Language use decisions apply not only to majority and minority languages in use in the school community but also to regional varieties of English, including those referred to by laypersons as "nonstandard dialects." Linguists studying language variation in the United States have found each regional dialect to be equally complex, grammatical, and purposeful, when compared with "standard" varieties of English (Heath, 1983; Wolfram & Christian, 1989). Assisting students with analyses of their own language use, through contrasting features of their community or regional variety and "standard" English, affirms students' self-identity and helps with the process of bidialectal acquisition (Ovando, 1993).

There is exciting research going on right now in a number of communities across the United States, where schools have formed partnerships with researchers who are committed to assist with this type of change process, crossing linguistic and cultural boundaries. When closer school-community relations are developed with low-income and minority communities, what is frequently revealed is a richer, more complex range of language use in the home, community, and professional life than was assumed by school personnel (Díaz, Moll & Mehan, 1986; Heath, 1986). In contrast, often researchers and teachers working together have been surprised to discover a very narrow, restricted focus of uses of language at school, in comparison to the richness of home and community nonformal learning.

By forging linkages between home and school, especially in regions of the U.S. where a large ethnolinguistic community has often experienced discrimination and resultant low academic achievement in school, students and staff working with researchers have expanded school curricula, recognizing the social and cultural nature of learning and language development. Such linkages have radically transformed school practices and students' academic achievement among African-Americans (Heath, 1983); Ethiopian-Americans, Haitian-Americans, and Portuguese-Americans (Rosebery, Warren & Conant, 1992; Warren, Rosebery & Conant, 1990); Hawaiian-Americans (Au & Jordan, 1981; Tharp & Gallimore, 1988; Vogt, Jordan & Tharp, 1993); Mexican-Americans (Ada, 1988; Delgado-Gaitán, 1987, 1990; González, Moll, Floyd-Tenery, Rivera, Rendón, Gonzales & Amanti, 1993; Moll & Díaz, 1993; Moll, Vélez-Ibáñez, Greenberg & Rivera, 1990), and Navajo-Americans (Rosier & Holm, 1980; Tharp & Gallimore, 1988; Tharp & Yamauchi, 1994; Vogt, Jordan & Tharp, 1993).

Cognitive & Academic Development

Cognitive Processes

Now that we have examined the subconscious linguistic processes that assist with acquisition of a second language, as well as social and cultural processes that have a strong influence, we are ready to explore the third major influence on second language acquisition for school—the cognitive dimension. Since cognitive processes take place inside the learner's head, you might naturally ask how these differ from linguistic processes. I am defining the cognitive dimension as those processes controlled by the brain that are within our conscious grasp; that is, they can be mediated by the learner and influenced by the teacher and the classroom setting. These are aspects of learning over which we have some control or we can consciously change, in contrast to the subconscious linguistic process that is ongoing, as long as learners are given opportunities for exposure to and use of the new language. I am also including development of all academic skills in all subject areas as a part of the cognitive dimension of second language acquisition for school.

THE IMPORTANCE OF THE COGNITIVE DIMENSION

This third dimension has been extensively debated by linguists who are developing major theories of second language acquisition. Some believe that the cognitive dimension is central to language acquisition, while others believe that it plays a minor role. I take the position that the cognitive dimension is equally as important as *the linguistic and sociocultural dimensions when examining second language acquisition* for school.

Krashen is probably one of the few linguists who has been "discovered" and popularized by language teachers, so I shall take a little space here to explain his position in comparison to other linguists. Krashen's position (1981, 1985) is that the innate, natural linguistic processes are central to second language acquisition. He bases his work on Noam Chomsky's theory in first language acquisition. Chomsky (1964, 1965) posited that we humans have an innate language acquisition device that is the central mechanism in first language acquisition. Krashen believes that we also use this innate capacity as the central process in second language acquisition. He distinguishes between subconscious language acquisition and formal learning in the language classroom, stating that the latter serves a very limited role, especially when it is focused on traditional teaching of language rules. Applying his theory to speak directly to teachers, Krashen and Terrell (1983; Terrell, 1981) developed the Natural Approach to language teaching, emphasizing natural language acquisition in the classroom with focus on activities that stimulate natural and meaningful language use. Interestingly, as Krashen has worked with bilingual educators over the past decade, while he still emphasizes natural language acquisition as the key, he has modified his position to incorporate the teaching of language through academic content, as a vehicle for natural language acquisition needed for school.

Other current theories of second language acquisition generally place cognitive processes in a more prominent or central role, such as theories by Ellis (1985, 1990), Wong Fillmore (1991b), McLaughlin (1987), and O'Malley and Chamot (1990). Ellis (1990) has contributed substantially to syntheses of the research base on the role that formal instruction plays in acquiring languages. He has shown that *teaching does make a difference, but the learner has to be devel-*

opmentally ready for the explicit knowledge presented and the language rules have to be teachable. While explicit knowledge helps the learner to notice language patterns, there is no automatic transfer to implicit knowledge, the acquired system. Thus Ellis concludes that *students need large amounts of meaning-focused practice of the language along with form-focused instruction at appropriate times.* Given a meaningful classroom context, as well as appropriate age and developmental stage of students, then conscious cognitive processes in a formal classroom setting can enhance acquisition of second language.

TYPES OF COGNITIVE PROCESSES

Wong Fillmore describes some of the cognitive processes that learners need to activate in order to stimulate the second language acquisition process:

> What learners must do with linguistic data is discover the system of rules the speakers of the language are following, synthesize this knowledge into a grammar, and then make it their own by internalizing it…. Learners apply a host of cognitive strategies and skills to deal with the task at hand: they have to make use of associative skills, memory, social knowledge, and inferential skills in trying to figure out what people are talking about. They use whatever analytical skills they have to figure out relationships between forms, functions, and meanings. They have to make use of memory, pattern recognition, induction, categorization, generalization, inference, and the like to figure out the structural principles by which the forms of the language can be combined, and meanings modified by changes and deletions.
>
> (Wong Fillmore, 1991b, pp. 56-57)

Wong Fillmore's theoretical model is based on dialogues over the past decade with many linguists and educators in interactive forums designed to develop the most comprehensive theory of second language acquisition. Her overview of second language acquisition combines all three processes—linguistic, social, and cognitive—into equally important dimensions.

McLaughlin (1987) provides a synthesis of some of the major cognitive processes involved in learning a second language, as support for his position that the cognitive dimension is central to language acquisition. He discusses the transfer of information to long-term memory (automaticity) and interpreting and reorganizing stored information with new information (restructuring) as applied to the process of learning a new language.

Although there is significant research in progress on the cognitive dimension in language acquisition, for the sake of brevity, I have chosen to limit this review to a few examples of current research on cognitive processes connected to second language acquisition. Two more aspects that we will examine briefly are cognitive style and learning strategy research.

COGNITIVE STYLES

Brown (1994) discusses theories of human learning and some of the mental processes used in language acquisition, as well as cognitive (or learning) styles and learning strategy research. He cautions us to be careful not to overgeneralize or oversimplify the complexity and diversity of human approaches to learning. When examining the influence of each of these factors on the language acquisition process, too often teachers receive a short training session on, for example, one or two learning style contrasts and then become zealous advocates of an oversimplified version which can lead to typing students into inappropriate categories. Probably the most-cited cognitive style contrast in the field of second language acquisition is field-independence/field-dependence; yet English learners seldom remain static on this dimension. Brown recommends that teachers be flexible in analyzing students' needs:

> Some would claim that styles are stable traits in adults. This is a questionable view. It would appear that individuals show general tendencies toward one style or another, but that differing contexts will evoke differing styles in one individual. Perhaps an "intelligent" and "successful" person is one who is "bicognitive"—one who can manipulate both ends of a style continuum.
>
> (Brown, 1994, p. 195)

So teachers can be open to a multitude of learning styles among the learners present in each classroom, by presenting instruction in many different ways.

LEARNING STRATEGIES

Another step teachers can take to enhance second language acquisition is to expand the range of learning strategies that students employ as they approach each classroom task, by consciously teaching learning strategies as part of the language acquisition process. Learning strategies are the techniques that we use to understand and retain information and to solve problems. Chamot and O'Malley (1986, 1987, 1994; O'Malley & Chamot, 1990) have conducted extensive research on second language learners and their learning strategy acquisition. They have shown that *when English learners receive instruction with explicit teaching of learning strategies, they become more efficient and effective learners in the second language* (Thomas, 1994). Chamot and O'Malley have identified three major types of learning strategies that are important in second language acquisition:

Metacognitive Strategies—planning for learning, monitoring one's own comprehension and production, and evaluating how well one has achieved a learning objective;

Cognitive Strategies—manipulating the material to be learned mentally (as in making images or elaborating) or physically (as in grouping items to be learned or taking notes); and

Social/Affective Strategies—either interacting with another person in order to assist learning, as in cooperative learning and asking questions for clarification, or using affective control to assist learning tasks.

(Chamot & O'Malley, 1994, pp. 60-61)

Teachers can assist students with learning strategy acquisition through interviews and think-aloud tasks that help identify what students already know, selecting new strategies to be taught, and helping students apply strategy use to new academic tasks. Details are provided for specific learning strategies to be taught in language classes and practical, meaningful ways to teach them in two very useful guides for teachers (Chamot & O'Malley, 1994; Oxford, 1990). Chamot & O'Malley's guide also includes detailed advice for teaching language through academic content.

LANGUAGE AND COGNITION

We are still in the process of discovering the complex relationship between language and cognition. But we must also remember the strong role that sociocultural influences play in language development. Earlier, we examined the crucial function of cognitive development in first language for the acquisition of second language for school. Vygotsky (1962, 1978) portrays in his theory how language expresses both external sociocultural reality and internal mental representations.

Thus, as children develop their ability to use language, they absorb more and more understanding of social situations and improve their thinking skills. This in turn allows them to learn how to control their own actions and thoughts. It is through a culturally bound and socially mediated process of language development that children construct mental frameworks (or schema) for perceiving the world around them. If language is a tool of thought, it follows that as children develop more complex thinking skills, the mental representations through which language and culture embody the child's world play a significant role.... If the culture of the classroom negates a child's first language and accompanying representations of the child's world, it is thus negating the tools the child has used to construct a basic cognitive framework.

(E. García, 1994, pp. 147-148)

Cognition, language, and culture are thus inextricably intertwined (Trueba, 1991). Students do best academically when we recognize that complex relationship and build on the knowledge base and experience that they bring to the classroom.

Academic Development

Now let's revisit Figure 1 on page 21. To understand the complex relationship between a student's first and second languages, the linguistic processes that assist with language acquisition, the sociocultural dimension, cognitive development, and academic development, one cannot easily separate first language from second language. It is all one process. Because language is the vehicle, or the means of expression, in all these domains, our language use must constantly continue to develop to higher and higher, more complex levels of proficiency and cognitive complexity. We have seen that cognitive development *must* continue uninterrupted throughout childhood. According to cognitive psychologists, we reach cognitive maturity around age 16, although some cognitive growth continues throughout our lifetime (Brown, 1994). Therefore, for children and adolescents, cognitive development *must* be continued in first language while second language is in process of development.

Likewise, academic development becomes more and more complex each year as we move into the high-technology information age of the 21st century. Given that ESL students miss several years of schooling while they are learning English, we are automatically relegating them to less academic and professional success when we do not provide instructional support for students to make up the lost academic time. That instructional support can most efficiently be provided in students' first language. Furthermore, teaching second language through academic content is an extremely effective way of providing for natural and meaningful second language acquisition.

EXAMPLES OF EFFECTIVE PROGRAMS FOR ACADEMIC DEVELOPMENT IN K-12 SETTINGS

Administrators and teachers have to make many decisions about the types of programs that we provide for all students, including English learners. Often we make these decisions with little information from research to guide us, and yet there is a growing research base that tells us a lot, as can be seen from the many studies cited in this monograph. In the popular press, you often hear reporters say that little has been learned about the most effective types of programs for ESL students, but this is not true. Generally when the statement is made, reporters are referring to the federally funded research, but the federal government has provided very little funding for research in our field. The large majority of the hundreds of high quality studies that have been conducted are carried out by university researchers and school practitioners, without special funding. What do these studies tell us about effective programs for English learners?

TWO-WAY DEVELOPMENTAL BILINGUAL EDUCATION. We have already discussed in some detail the important reasons for students' academic development in first language. This is a program decision that is especially crucial for students in Grades K-12, because children and young adolescents are still developing cognitively throughout these school years. And yet the United States has not experienced enormous success with improving the academic achievement of language minority students through the most common bilingual program model—transitional (or "early-exit") bilingual education programs. In transitional bilingual classes, students are provided academic development in first language for 2-3 years (most often in the lower elementary school grades), during which time they are isolated from their English-speaking peers for part or sometimes all of the school day. In general, transitional bilingual classes have subconsciously been relegated to a lower or remedial status (Spener, 1988). Although transitional classes appear to have potential for success, the chief problem is the way they are perceived by school staff and students, as well as the limited number of years of first language academic development (Collier, 1989b; Ovando & Collier, 1995).

In contrast, *the most consistently successful academic achievement has occurred in two-way developmental bilingual education programs, where English speakers are schooled together with language minority students, and the English-speaking parents, along with language minority parents, can affirm the importance of learning in two languages* (California Department of Education, 1991; Collier, 1989a, 1989b, 1992a, 1992c; O. García, 1991; Genesee, 1987;

Krashen & Biber, 1988; Lindholm, 1990, 1991; Thomas & Collier, 1995). The chief difference between this type of program and other types of bilingual programs is that majority and minority students are integrated together and consequently the program tends to achieve a high social status. *When majority parents believe that the program is great for their own children, attitudes toward the program can change dramatically. Perceptions are powerful in academic success.*

For those readers who are new to this field, I need to explain the two names for this program model. "Two-way" is the older term used by bilingual educators in the U.S. first implementing programs in the 1960s. Stern (1963) first introduced the term "one-way" bilingual education as an instructional model for one language minority group and "two-way" bilingual education as a program where majority and minority students study together academically in two languages. When the U.S. federal government provided funding for this program model, the federal legislation re-named the model "developmental bilingual education" to emphasize the developmental nature of cognitive, academic, and linguistic development and to eradicate the perception that bilingual education is remedial in nature. *Students do not "exit" from this program model, in contrast to transitional bilingual education, because students are educated in an integrated context, through the standard school curriculum, in an academically rigorous classroom.*

What are other important program characteristics that appear to make a two-way developmental bilingual program successful? *Integrated schooling, with English speakers and language minority students learning each others' languages, provides for more harmonious intergroup relations* (González, 1979). An English-speaking graduate of a two-way bilingual program put it this way: "Aside from the obvious advantage of learning a second language, I learned a great deal of respect and patience for non-English speakers. Because we struggled alongside one another to learn one another's languages, we learned to appreciate one another in a way that, otherwise, we might not have" (Collier, 1989a). Fishman (1976, pp. 9-19) presents the case to language majority parents even more passionately as

> a serious quest for a better society and a saner world. For bilingual and bicultural education to succeed in its greater cultural mission, it must be available to all...to learn to handle multiple loyalties and membership constructively, openly, proudly, without suppression, without shame, without conflict, without tension.

Another big advantage for stimulation of the natural second language acquisition process is that *students in a two-way bilingual program* tend to develop a deeper level of proficiency in both languages, because they *serve as peer teachers in a highly interactive classroom* (Lindholm, 1990; Oller, 1993). Second language acquisition research has clearly demonstrated that the most important source of input in second language development comes from same-age peers, and peers are more important than the teacher as a model for the new language. Furthermore, *deep proficiency develops in both languages, because the focus is on* **meaningful use of the two languages through academic content across the curriculum.**

Still another advantage of a two-way developmental program is *the change in the sociocultural context in which students are schooled, with more equal status given to the two languages, creating self-confidence among language minority students, within an additive bilingual context for maximum cognitive and academic development.* In this type of program, often schools report healthy parent involvement among both language minority and English-speaking parents, resulting in *closer home-school collaboration.*

In our current research (Thomas & Collier, 1995), we found that two-way bilingual education provided for students at the elementary school level is the most promising program model for the long-term academic achievement of language minority students. It is the only program where language minority students consistently maintain their academic success throughout high school, even though they may not have the opportunity to continue to develop their first language academically once they reach secondary school. The confidence that language minority students gain in classes where they are challenged with meaningful academic instruction through two languages is unparalleled. By adding to that the stimulus of working academically with English-speaking peers, learning appears to accelerate, as the two groups serve as peer tutors for each other.

MAINTENANCE OR "LATE-EXIT" BILINGUAL EDUCATION. Furthermore, in maintenance or "late-exit" bilingual education programs that continue through the upper elementary grades to provide first language academic instruction, along with balanced second language academic instruction, language minority students can also maintain their academic success at secondary level, even when the instruction in middle and high school is delivered exclusively through second language (Krashen & Biber, 1988; Medina, Saldate & Mishra, 1985; Thomas & Collier, 1995). Academic knowledge gained in first language transfers to second language. Thus, the more students have received high-quality education in first language, the deeper their knowledge base across the two languages. Even though language minority students may be segregated from English speakers in this type of program, they are able to build the self-confidence and academic skills needed to succeed in secondary school contexts all in second language.

EFFECTIVE INSTRUCTIONAL PRACTICES FOR STUDENTS OF ALL AGES

But academic development of first language is not enough. Furthermore, many programs can deceive us by using the name of a model program but having few of the essential characteristics that provide for an effective schooling context. Thus our discussion of effective schooling for language minority students needs to shift to the essential elements of instructional practices, regardless of the name given to a specific program. The following discussion provides an overview of research findings from recent studies that have identified effective instructional practices with language minority students of all ages.

THEMATIC, INTERDISCIPLINARY INSTRUCTION. *Teaching second language through meaningful academic content across the curriculum (language arts, mathematics, science, social studies,...) is now considered crucial to second language academic success* (Cocking & Mestre, 1988; Crandall, 1987; Fathman, Quinn & Kessler, 1992; Mohan, 1986; Short, 1991). In the 1960s and 1970s our field focused on teaching language first and then later introducing students to academic content. Now we know that we cannot afford the lost time, since it takes many years for ESL students to reach academic proficiency in the second language (Collier, 1987, 1988, 1989c, 1992a, 1992c ; Collier & Thomas, 1988, 1989; Thomas & Collier, 1995). We know from research on bilingual education for language majority students (labeled "immersion education" by the Canadians), as well as research on bilingual education for language minority students, that second language can successfully be taught simultaneously with academic content (Collier, 1993a). There is no reason to hold students back.

Thematic approaches to teaching provide a meaningful framework for exploring something of great interest to students and teachers, through an interdisciplinary journey that develops academic skills and learning strategies in each content area, through in-depth problem-posing and problem-solving. Teacher and students together choose themes to be developed and together explore knowledge gathering and knowledge producing. Themes generally focus on something that is a universal human experience, helping students connect to their past knowledge and experiences. Several studies have identified thematic, interdisciplinary teaching as a crucial ingredient in effective instruction with ESL students of all ages (Au, 1993; Brinton, Snow & Wesche, 1989; E.García, 1988; Goodman & Wilde, 1992; Henderson & Landesman, 1992).

MULTICULTURAL, GLOBAL PERSPECTIVES. Many research findings in language minority education have clearly established that students learn best when lessons connect to their past experiences (Au, 1993; Genesee, 1994; Tharp & Gallimore, 1988; Trueba, 1991; Trueba, Guthrie & Au, 1981). *Activation of students' prior knowledge is considered the first step in any meaningful instructional activity* (Chamot & O'Malley, 1994; Freeman & Freeman, 1992; E.García, 1994). However, too many teachers interpret multicultural perspectives to mean emphasizing a few points about other nations or ethnic groups, or celebrating holidays and heroes of other cultures, which often degenerates into superficial glimpses that lead to stereotyping and terribly inaccurate misinformation. *When a class is very diverse, a more appropriate multicultural perspective focuses on examining how we humans lead our lives everyday, reflecting on variations in other regions in response to each geographic and social environment, exploring the complexity of the human spirit and mind.* In a teaching context that is mostly bicultural, instruction can successfully incorporate particular bicultural patterns of human experience of the two groups in that region, such as effective instructional practices discovered in working with Hawaiian-Americans (Au, 1993; Tharp & Gallimore, 1988), Mexican-Americans (Ada, 1988; Delgado-Gaitán, 1987, 1990; Díaz, Moll & Mehan, 1986; González, Moll, Floyd-Tenery, Rivera, Rendón, Gonzales & Amanti, 1992; Moll & Díaz, 1993), and Navajo-Americans (Tharp & Yamauchi, 1994).

COLLABORATIVE, INTERACTIVE LEARNING. In the research on effective instructional practices with language minority students, it is very clear that when students and teachers work as partners in the learning process, rather than the teacher serving as the dispenser of knowledge, then the magic truly begins to happen (Au, 1993; Enright & McCloskey, 1988; Faltis, 1993; Freeman & Freeman, 1992; Gaies, 1985; E. García, 1988, 1994; Genesee, 1994; Goodman & Wilde, 1992; Hamayan, 1993; Harmin, 1994; Holt, 1993; Holt, Chips & Wallace, 1992; Johnson & Johnson, 1986; Kagan, 1986; Malamah-Thomas, 1987; McCaleb, 1994; Richard-Amato, 1988; Richard-Amato & Snow, 1992; Scarcella & Oxford, 1992; Shoemaker & Shoemaker, 1991; Solís, 1989; Tharp & Gallimore, 1988; Tharp & Yamauchi, 1994; Tinajero & Ada, 1993; Valdez Pierce, 1991). This shift in the teacher-student relationship is a return to the thinking of two classic philosophers of education—John Dewey, U.S. educator of the early 20th century, and Paulo Freire, a world-renowned educator who is now the Minister of Education in Brazil. For both Dewey and Freire, *student-centered, discovery learning is the key. The teacher serves in an important role as guide and facilitator, helping to structure the ways that students and teacher will explore new knowledge or pose problems to be solved or acted upon* (Freire, 1985; Freire & Macedo, 1987; Shor & Freire, 1987). Given the knowledge explosion in each field, we must prepare students to know how to gain access to new knowledge and to apply, evaluate, and solve problems based on changing knowledge (Cummins, 1986a, 1989a, 1989b).

Since in an interactive classroom, the teacher is no longer the authority figure around whom all activity is centered, *teachers need to structure class activities so that all students are involved in intensive learning.* We have already discussed the importance of *peer interaction to stimulate the natural second language acquisition process* as one of the reasons for collaborative learning (Faltis, 1993; Gaies, 1985; Malamah-Thomas, 1987; Shoemaker & Shoemaker, 1991; Wong Fillmore, 1989, 1991b). Other reasons for creating a classroom in which students spend considerable time working in small groups or pairs are that *cooperative learning structures result in dramatic academic gains, especially for students at risk* (Jacob & Mattson, 1990; Johnson & Johnson, 1986; Kagan, 1986; Slavin, 1988); that *cooperative learning helps develop prosocial skills;* and that *students need to be prepared for an increasingly interdependent workplace* (Kagan, 1992). Analyzing instructional practices in a high-achieving language minority school, García found that

> it was during student-student interactions that most higher order cognitive and linguistic discourse was observed. Students asked each other hard questions and challenged each other's answers more readily than they did in interactions with the teachers. Moreover, students were likely to seek assistance from other students and were successful in obtaining it.
>
> (E.García, 1991, p. 4)

Cooperative learning (generally referred to as collaborative learning in higher education contexts) is a strategy for classroom management and structuring of curricular materials that provides the teacher with a wide range of techniques for small group work so that students remain on task and prosocial skills are developed. Given the multiple learning styles present in any classroom, the diversity of needs of learners, the varied levels of proficiency in the language of instruction, and the varied academic knowledge represented, teachers can organize the class to respond to these needs by alternating classroom structures between total-class, small-group, pair, and individual learning. Cooperative learning structures assist with heterogeneous small-group and pair work in which students share responsibility for completing each academic task. Several excellent resource books provide a wealth of practical teaching strategies to promote interactive learning in classes with language minority students (e.g. for K-12 contexts: Holt, 1993; Holt, Chips & Wallace, 1992; Kagan, 1992; for higher education contexts: Johnson, Johnson & Smith, 1991).

CHALLENGING STUDENTS COGNITIVELY. I have discussed at some length the importance of uninterrupted cognitive development in first language. This can take place wherever possible, in bilingual classes, weekend schools, with parents, and through peer and sibling tutoring. But *along with cognitive development in first language, development of thinking skills should also be consciously developed in ESL classes of all levels.* If you think that we need to wait until students are ready, go visit a first grade two-way developmental bilingual class, where teachers don't waste any time getting down to meaningful, challenging academic work in math and science in the very first weeks, teaching attributes, relationships, classification, environmental issues, science experiments, and other complex curricular concepts *through the second language,* to beginners. During the English instruction, the English-speaking students are peer assistants, and during the Spanish (or Chinese or...) instruction, the Spanish-speaking students are expert assistants. Lots of extracontextual clues to meaning make it possible, and the students know they are respected and challenged.

To challenge students cognitively involves taking the standard curriculum or the course objectives as your base, for your class to explore interesting and meaningful material at the deepest levels of knowledge that you can reach. Learning can be organized to assist each student with basic skills to be mastered through meaningful, thematic work that simultaneously addresses both language and academic content. Learning strategy acquisition also becomes a conscious and meaningful activity (Chamot & O'Malley, 1994; Oxford, 1990).

Finally, let's not forget technology as an integral aspect of cognitively complex learning in the late 20th century. Given the explosion of the uses of technology in the workplace, home, and school, our students need access to greatly varied uses of instructional multimedia—audiocassette players, video equipment, cellular phones, compact disc players, cameras, computers, interactive videodisc players, and other electronic devices bound to continue to appear in the near future. Using computers in instruction can expand students' language and academic skills through use of word processing software, spread sheets, database software, communications programs, graphics packages, hypermedia, and access to telecommunications such as electronic mail. However, students passively watching a movie for an hour, or working on mindless drill and practice exercises on the computer, is not considered effective instruction. *Technology must be integrated in a meaningful way into interactive, cognitively complex lessons through second language* (Ahmad, Corbett, Rogers & Sussex, 1984; Gaer & Ferenz, 1993; Hardisty & Windeatt, 1989; Lonergan, 1984; O'Neil, 1993; Penfield, 1987; Susser, 1993).

TEACHING READING AND WRITING. Throughout our lives, we are always in the process of continuing acquisition of the written language, whether it is our first or second language. *Today we teach reading and writing as a long-term, developmental process, that is never-ending. Thus reading and writing are an integral part of any academic course or subject area, and all our students, native and non-native speakers, have reached many different stages in the reading/ writing process.* To give students continuing responsibility for their personal growth, we constantly challenge them to read and write more and more. Our overall goal is to enable students to use and enjoy reading and writing "to learn about and interpret the world and to reflect upon themselves in relation to people and events around them;...and to explain, analyze, argue about, and act upon the world" (Hudelson, 1994, p. 130). Au (1993) emphasizes *the importance of constructing meaning through written language by making students' background experiences cen-*

tral to the literacy process, using culturally responsive instruction. Other researchers in ESL reading and writing emphasize the importance of understanding that *students of all ages best acquire reading and writing skills through many varied interactive, collaborative activities with peers, cross-age tutors, and adults.* Many wonderful sources provide extensive discussions on effective instructional practices for teaching reading and writing through second language (Adamson, 1993; Cantoni-Harvey, 1987, 1992; Carson & Leki, 1993; Cook & Urzua, 1993; Delgado-Gaitán, 1990; Enright & McCloskey, 1988; Freeman & Freeman, 1992; Goodman & Wilde, 1992; Heath & Mangiola, 1991; Johnson & Roen, 1989; Peyton, 1990; Peyton & Reid, 1990; Rigg &Enright, 1986; Samway, 1992; Scarcella & Oxford, 1992; Tharp & Gallimore, 1988; Tinajero & Ada, 1993; Williams & Snipper, 1990). This brief summary is too short to do justice to the rich research knowledge base in this area.

EFFECTIVE SCHOOL MANAGEMENT PRACTICES

Second language acquisition research also speaks to principals and other educational administrators regarding the sociocultural climate present in an educational setting. The total school context is a critical factor influencing language minority students' academic achievement. Earlier we discussed some examples of sociocultural influences. Within the public school context, the current school reform movement has potential to address a number of sociocultural concerns, if the dialogue is thoughtful and reflects research findings from language minority education (National Coalition of Advocates for Students, 1988, 1991).

For example, *one aspect of school reform—shared decision-making, or collaborative leadership—can strongly assist language minority students' academic achievement when diverse groups are represented and they can successfully collaborate* (McKeon & Malarz, 1991), as has been shown in the "accelerated schools" model for at risk students (Rothman, 1991). In this model, the entire school community—teachers, parents, students, and administrators—are actively involved in curricular changes and meaningful connections to the culturally diverse communities the school serves.

Another major change in the administrative structure of schools is the movement toward *eliminating tracking and ability grouping* (Gamoran, 1990; Oakes, 1985, 1992; Wheelock, 1992), *through development of more team teaching, use of heterogeneous cooperative learning structures, and exploration of experiential, discovery learning at a high cognitive level, even when basic skills are an integral goal of coursework, with high expectations of all students* (Collier, 1992b; E. García, 1988, 1994; Rivera & Zehler, 1990). Minicucci & Olsen (1992) found that even when secondary schools work very hard to provide an appropriate learning environment for language minority students, the structural rigidity of departmentalized secondary schools works against students' needs. The middle school reform movement, with increasing flexibility in school structures, has been able to respond better to diverse needs of learners. An urgent need in reform at secondary school level is to assist language minority students with access to the core curriculum needed to graduate from high school.

Other issues center around providing an appropriate school climate. *In schools with strong support for language minority students, researchers have found that administrators and all school staff have a commitment to empowering language minority students through providing bilingual/bicultural role models, serving as community advocates, providing bicultural counseling support with knowledge of postsecondary opportunities, being available after school and organizing meaningful extracurricular activities, and creating a school climate that values cultural and linguistic diversity* (Lucas, Henze & Donato, 1990; Tikunoff, Ward, van Broekhuizen, Romero, Castañeda, Lucas & Katz, 1991; Valdez Pierce, 1991).

Conclusion

Language minority students are an invaluable resource. They are our key to the future. By the turn of the century, they will be at least 25 percent of the newly entering workforce in the U.S. Past immigrant groups have provided a constant stimulus for new ideas as well as strong commitment to the ideals upon which the U.S. is founded. All of the most recently arrived groups have shown the same kind of persistent hope that they can succeed in a new life here, and they want to take responsibility for their own lives. To leave home and start life over in a new land involves great risk taking.

We educators can create blocks to language minorities' progress through continuation of school policies that reinforce the inequities and that widen the gap between majority and minority. Or we can examine the research findings and discover that the changes needed for language minority students to succeed academically will benefit *all* students. It is our choice. Why not provide a meaningful, motivating academic environment, for everyone to succeed?

References

Ada, A.F. (1988). The Pájaro Valley experience: Working with Spanish-speaking parents to develop children's reading and writing skills through the use of children's literature. In T. Skutnabb-Kangas & J. Cummins (Eds.), *Minority education: From shame to struggle* (pp. 223-238). Clevedon, England: Multilingual Matters.

Adamson, H.D. (1993). *Academic competence: Theory and classroom practice: Preparing ESL students for content courses.* New York: Longman.

Ahmad, K., Corbett, G., Rogers, M., & Sussex, R. (1985). *Computers, language learning and language teaching* Cambridge: Cambridge University Press.

Allwright, D., & Bailey, K.M. (1991). *Focus on the language classroom: An introduction to classroom research for language teachers.* Cambridge: Cambridge University Press.

Arnberg, L. (1987). *Raising children bilingually: The pre-school years.* Clevedon, England: Multilingual Matters.

Au, K.H. (1993). *Literacy instruction in multicultural settings.* Fort Worth, TX: Harcourt Brace Jovanovich.

Au, K.H., & Jordan, C. (1981). Teaching reading to Hawaiian children: Finding a culturally appropriate solution. In H.T. Trueba, G.P. Guthrie, & K.H. Au (Eds.), *Culture and the bilingual classroom: Studies in classroom ethnography* (pp. 139-152). Cambridge, MA: Newbury House.

Baker, C. (1988). *Key issues in bilingualism and bilingual education.* Clevedon, England: Multilingual Matters.

Baker, C. (1993). *Foundations of bilingual education and bilingualism.* Clevedon, England: Multilingual Matters.

Berko Gleason, J. (1993). *The development of language* (3rd ed.). New York: Macmillan.

Bialystok, E. (Ed.). (1991). *Language processing in bilingual children.* Cambridge: Cambridge University Press.

Brinton, D.M., Snow, M.A., & Wesche, M.B. (1989). *Content-based second language instruction.* Cambridge, MA: Newbury House.

Brown, H.D. (1994). *Principles of language learning and teaching* (3rd ed.). Englewood Cliffs, NJ: Prentice Hall Regents.

California Department of Education. (1984). *Studies on immersion education: A collection for United States educators.* Sacramento, CA: Author.

California Department of Education. (1991). Los Angeles Unified achieves excellence with bilingual approach. *Bilingual Education Office Outreach,* 2(2), 12-13, 15.

Cantoni-Harvey, G. (1987). *Content-area language instruction: Approaches and strategies.* Reading, MA: Addison-Wesley.

Cantoni-Harvey, G. (1992). Facilitating the reading process. In P.A. Richard-Amato & M.A. Snow (Eds.), *The multicultural classroom: Readings for content-area teachers* (pp. 175-197). New York: Longman.

Caplan, N., Choy, M.H., & Whitmore, J.K. (1992). Indochinese refugee families and academic achievement. *Scientific American,* 266(2), 36-42.

Carson, J.G., & Leki, I. (Eds.). (1993). *Reading in the composition classroom: Second language perspectives.* Boston: Heinle & Heinle.

Chamot, A.U., & O'Malley, J.M. (1986). *A cognitive academic language learning approach: An ESL content-based curriculum.* Washington, DC: National Clearinghouse for Bilingual Education.

Chamot, A.U., & O'Malley, J.M. (1987). The cognitive academic language learning approach: A bridge to the mainstream. *TESOL Quarterly,* 21, 227-249.

Chamot, A.U., & O'Malley, J.M. (1994). *The CALLA handbook: Implementing the Cognitive Academic Language Learning Approach.* Reading, MA: Addison-Wesley.

Chaudron, C. (1988). *Second language classrooms: Research on teaching and learning.* Cambridge: Cambridge University Press.

Chomsky, N. (1964). *Current issues in linguistic theory.* The Hague: Mouton.

Chomsky, N. (1965). *Aspects of the theory of syntax.* Cambridge, MA: MIT Press.

Chu, H.S. (1981). *Testing instruments for reading skills: English and Korean (Grades 1-3).* Fairfax, VA: Center for Bilingual/Multicultural/ESL Education, George Mason University.

Cocking, R.R., & Mestre, J.P. (Eds.). (1988). *Linguistic and cultural influences on learning mathematics.* Hillsdale, NJ: Lawrence Erlbaum.

Coelho, E. (1994). Social integration of immigrant and refugee children. In F. Genesee (Ed.), *Educating second language children* (pp. 301-327). Cambridge: Cambridge University Press.

Collier, V.P. (1981). A sociological case study of bilingual education and its effects on the schools and the community. In *Outstanding dissertations in bilingual education: Recognized by the National Advisory Council on Bilingual Education.* Washington, DC: National Clearinghouse for Bilingual Education. (Doctoral dissertation available from University of Southern California, 304 pp.)

Collier, V.P. (1985). University models for ESL and bilingual teacher training. In *Issues in English language development* (pp. 81-90). Washington, DC: National Clearinghouse for Bilingual Education.

Collier, V.P. (1986). Cross-cultural policy issues in minority and majority parent involvement. In *Issues of parent involvement and literacy* (pp. 73-78). Washington, DC: National Clearinghouse for Bilingual Education.

Collier, V.P. (1987). Age and rate of acquisition of second language for academic purposes. *TESOL Quarterly, 21,* 617-641.

Collier, V.P. (1988). *The effect of age on acquisition of a second language for school.* Washington, DC: National Clearinghouse for Bilingual Education.

Collier, V.P. (1989a). *Academic achievement, attitudes, and occupations among graduates of two-way bilingual classes.* Paper presented at the annual meeting of the American Educational Research Association, San Francisco, CA.

Collier, V.P. (1989b). Education: Bilingualism. In *1989 Americana Annual/Encyclopedia Year Book.* Danbury, CT: Grolier.

Collier, V.P. (1989c). How long? A synthesis of research on academic achievement in second language. *TESOL Quarterly, 23,* 509-531.

Collier, V.P. (1991). *Language minority students and higher education: Access, programs, and policies.* Trenton, NJ: New Jersey Department of Higher Education.

Collier, V.P. (1992a). The Canadian bilingual immersion debate: A synthesis of research findings. *Studies in Second Language Acquisition, 14,* 87-97.

Collier, V.P. (1992b). Reforming teacher education. In *Proceedings of the Second National Research Symposium on Limited-English-Proficient Student Issues: Focus on evaluation and measurement* (Vol. 2, pp. 417-421). Washington, DC: Office of Bilingual Education and Minority Language Affairs, U.S. Department of Education.

Collier, V.P. (1992c). A synthesis of studies examining long-term language minority student data on academic achievement. *Bilingual Research Journal, 16*(1-2), 187-212.

Collier, V.P. (1993a). [Review of Ofelia García (Ed.), *Bilingual education: Focusschrift in honor of Joshua A. Fishman* (Vol. 1)]. Language in Society.

Collier, V.P., & Thomas, W.P. (1988, April). *Acquisition of cognitive-academic second language proficiency: A six-year study.* Paper presented at the annual meeting of the American Educational Research Association, New Orleans, LA.

Collier, V.P., & Thomas, W.P. (1989). How quickly can immigrants become proficient in school English? *Journal of Educational Issues of Language Minority Students, 5,* 26-38.

Condon, J.C., & Yousef, F.S. (1975). An introduction to intercultural communication. Indianapolis: Bobbs-Merrill.

Connor, U., & Kaplan, R.B. (Eds.). (1987). *Writing across languages: Analysis of L2 text.* Reading, MA: Addison-Wesley.

Cook, B., & Urzua, C. (1993). *The literacy club: A cross-age tutoring/paired reading project.* Washington, DC: National Clearinghouse for Bilingual Education.

Crandall, J. (Ed.). (1987). *ESL through content-area instruction: Mathematics, science, social studies.* Englewood Cliffs, NJ: Prentice Hall Regents.

Crawford, J. (1992a). *Hold your tongue: Bilingualism and the politics of "English only."* Reading, MA: Addison-Wesley.

Crawford, J. (Ed.). (1992b). *Language loyalties: A source book on the official English controversy.* Chicago: University of Chicago Press.

Cummins, J. (1976). The influence of bilingualism on cognitive growth: A synthesis of research findings and explanatory hypotheses. *Working Papers on Bilingualism, 9,* 1-43.

Cummins, J. (1977). Cognitive factors associated with the attainment of intermediate levels of bilingual skills. *Modern Language Journal, 61,* 3-12.

Cummins, J. (1979). Cognitive/academic language proficiency, linguistic interdependence, the optimal age question, and some other matters. *Working Papers on Bilingualism,* 19, 197-205.

Cummins, J. (1981). The role of primary language development in promoting educational success for language minority students. In *Schooling and language minority students* (pp. 3-49). Sacramento, CA: California Department of Education.

Cummins, J. (1986a). Empowering minority students: A framework for intervention. *Harvard Education Review,* 56, 18-36.

Cummins, J. (1986b). Language proficiency and academic achievement. In J. Cummins & M. Swain, *Bilingualism in education* (pp. 138-161). New York: Longman.

Cummins, J. (1989a). *Empowering minority students.* Sacramento, CA: California Association for Bilingual Education.

Cummins, J. (1989b). The sanitized curriculum: Educational disempowerment in a nation at risk. In D.M. Johnson & D.H. Roen (Eds.), *Richness in writing: Empowering ESL students* (pp. 19-38). New York: Longman.

Cummins, J. (1991). Interdependence of first- and second-language proficiency in bilingual children. In E. Bialystok (Ed.), *Language processing in bilingual children* (pp. 70-89). Cambridge: Cambridge University Press.

Cummins, J. (1992). Bilingual education and English immersion: The Ramírez report in theoretical perspective. *Bilingual Research Journal,* 16(1-2), 91-104.

Cummins, J., & Swain, M. (1986). *Bilingualism in education.* New York: Longman.

Delgado-Gaitán, C. (1987). Parent perceptions of school: Supportive environments for children. In H.T. Trueba (Ed.), *Success or failure? Learning and the language minority student* (pp. 131-155). Cambridge, MA: Newbury House.

Delgado-Gaitán, C. (1990). *Literacy for empowerment: The role of parents in children's education.* New York: Falmer Press.

de Villiers, J.G., & de Villiers, P.A. (1978). *Language acquisition.* Cambridge, MA: Harvard University Press.

Díaz, R.M., & Klingler, C. (1991). Towards an explanatory model of the interaction between bilingualism and cognitive development. In E. Bialystok (Ed.), *Language processing in bilingual children* (pp. 167-192). Cambridge: Cambridge University Press.

Díaz, S., Moll, L.C., & Mehan, H. (1986). Sociocultural resources in instruction: A context-specific approach. In *Beyond language: Social and cultural factors in schooling language minority students* (pp. 187-230). Sacramento, CA: California Department of Education.

Dolson, D.P. (1985). The effects of Spanish home language use on the scholastic performance of Hispanic pupils. *Journal of Multilingual Multicultural Development,* 6, 135-155.

Dolson, D.P., & Mayer, J. (1992). Longitudinal study of three program models for language-minority students: A critical examination of reported findings. *Bilingual Research Journal,* 16(1-2), 105-157.

Dulay, H., & Burt, M. (1980). The relative proficiency of limited English proficient students. In J.E. Alatis (Ed.), *Current issues in bilingual education* (pp. 181-200). Washington, DC: Georgetown University Press.

Dulay, H., Burt, M., & Krashen, S. (1982). *Language two.* New York: Oxford University Press.

Duncan, S.E., & De Avila, E.A. (1979). Bilingualism and cognition: Some recent findings. *NABE Journal,* 4(1), 15-20.

Eisenhart, M.A., & Graue, M.E. (1993). Constructing cultural differences and educational achievement in schools. In E. Jacob & C. Jordan (Eds.), *Minority education: Anthropological perspectives* (pp. 165-179). Norwood, NJ: Ablex.

Ellis, R. (1985). *Understanding second language acquisition.* Oxford: Oxford University Press.

Ellis, R. (1990). *Instructed second language acquisition.* Oxford: Blackwell.

Enright, D.S., & McCloskey, M.L. (1988). *Integrating English: Developing English language and literacy in the multilingual classroom.* Reading, MA: Addison-Wesley.

Faltis, C.J. (1993). *Joinfostering: Adapting teaching strategies for the multilingual classroom.* New York: Macmillan.

Fathman, A.K., Quinn, M.E., & Kessler, C. (1992). *Teaching science to English learners, Grades 4-8.* Program Information Guide Series, No. 11. Washington, DC: National Clearinghouse for Bilingual Education.

Fishman, J.A. (1976). *Bilingual education: An international sociological perspective.* Cambridge, MA: Newbury House.

Freeman, Y.S., & Freeman, D.E. (1992). *Whole language for second language learners.* Portsmouth, NH: Heinemann.

Freire, P. (1985). *The politics of education: Culture, power and liberation.* New York: Bergin & Garvey.

Freire, P., & Macedo, D. (1987). *Literacy: Reading the word and the world.* South New York: Bergin & Garvey.

Gaer, S., & Ferenz, K. (1993). Telecommunications and interactive writing projects. *CAELL Journal,* 4(2), 2-5.

Gaies, S.J. (1985). *Peer involvement in language learning.* Englewood Cliffs, NJ: Prentice Hall Regents.

Gamoran, A. (1990). How tracking affects achievement: Research and recommendations. *National Center on Effective Secondary Schools Newsletter,* 5(1), 2-6.

García, E. (1988). *Effective schooling for language minority students.* Washington, DC: National Clearing-house for Bilingual Education.

García, E. (1991). *Education of linguistically and culturally diverse students: Effective instructional practices.* Santa Cruz, CA: National Center for Research on Cultural Diversity and Second Language Learning.

García, E. (1993). Language, culture, and education. In L. Darling-Hammond (Ed.), *Review of research in education* (Vol. 19, pp. 51-98). Washington, DC: American Educational Research Association.

García, E. (1994). *Understanding and meeting the challenge of student cultural diversity.* Boston: Houghton Mifflin.

García, O. (Ed.). (1991). *Bilingual education: Focusschrift in honor of Joshua A. Fishman,* Vol. 1. Amsterdam: John Benjamins.

Gass, S., & Madden, C. (Eds.). (1985). *Input in second language acquisition.* Cambridge, MA: Newbury House.

Genesee, F. (1987). *Learning through two languages: Studies of immersion and bilingual education.* Cambridge, MA: Newbury House.

Genesee, F. (Ed.). (1994). *Educating second language children: The whole child, the whole curriculum, the whole community.* Cambridge: Cambridge University Press.

González, J. (1979). *Bilingual education in the integrated school.* Washington, DC: National Clearinghouse for Bilingual Education.

González, N., Moll, L., Floyd-Tenery, M., Rivera, A., Rendón, P., Gonzales, R., & Amanti, C. (1993). *Teacher research on funds of knowledge: Learning from households.* Santa Cruz, CA: National Center for Research on Cultural Diversity and Second Language Learning.

Goodluck, H. (1991). *Language acquisition.* Oxford: Blackwell.

Goodman, Y.M., & Wilde, S. (Eds.) (1992). *Literacy events in a community of young writers.* New York: Teachers College Press.

Goodz, N. (1994). Interactions between parents and children in bilingual families. In F. Genesee (Ed.), *Educating second language children* (pp. 61-81). Cambridge: Cambridge University Press.

Grosjean, F. (1982). *Life with two languages: An introduction to bilingualism.* Cambridge, MA: Harvard University Press.

Hakuta, K. (1986). *Mirror of language: The debate on bilingualism.* New York: Basic Books.

Hakuta, K. (1987). The second-language learner in the context of the study of language acquisition. In P. Homel, M. Palij, & D. Aaronson (Eds.), *Childhood bilingualism: Aspects of linguistic, cognitive, and social development* (pp. 31-55). Hillsdale, NJ: Lawrence Erlbaum.

Hamayan, E.V. (1993). Current trends in ESL curriculum. In *English as a second language curriculum resource handbook: A practical guide for K-12 ESL programs* (pp. 16-34). Millwood, NY: Kraus International.

Harding, E., & Riley, P. (1986). *The bilingual family: A handbook for parents.* Cambridge: Cambridge University Press.

Hardisty, D., & Windeatt, S. (1989). *CALL.* Oxford: Oxford University Press.

Harley, B. (1986). *Age in second language acquisition.* Clevedon, England: Multilingual Matters.

Harley, B., Allen, P., Cummins, J., & Swain, M. (Eds.). (1990). *The development of second language proficiency.* Cambridge: Cambridge University Press.

Harmin, M. (1994). *Inspiring active learning: A handbook for teachers.* Alexandria, VA: Association for Supervision and Curriculum Development.

Hatch, E. (1978). *Second language acquisition.* Cambridge, MA: Newbury House.

Hatch, E. (1983). *Psycholinguistics: A second language perspective.* Cambridge, MA: Newbury House.

Heath, S.B. (1983). *Ways with words: Language, life, and work in communities and classrooms.* Cambridge: Cambridge University Press.

Heath, S.B. (1986). Sociocultural contexts of language development. In *Beyond language: Social and cultural factors in schooling language minority students* (pp. 143-186). Sacramento, CA: California Department of Education.

Heath, S.B., & Mangiola, L. (1991). *Children of promise: Literate activity in linguistically and culturally diverse classrooms.* Washington, DC: National Education Association.

Henderson, R.W., & Landesman, E.M. (1992). *Mathematics and middle school students of Mexican descent: The effects of thematically integrated instruction.* Santa Cruz, CA: National Center for Research on Cultural Diversity and Second Language Learning.

Hernández-Chávez, E. (1977). Meaningful bilingual-bicultural education: A fairytale. *NABE Journal,* 1(3), 49-54.

Hernández-Chávez, E. (1984). The inadequacy of English immersion education as an educational approach for language minority students in the United States. In *Studies on immersion education: A collection for United States educators* (pp. 144-183). Sacramento, CA: California Department of Education.

Holt, D. (Ed.). (1993). *Cooperative learning: A response to linguistic and cultural diversity.* McHenry, IL: Delta Systems.

Holt, D., Chips, B., & Wallace, D. (1992). *Cooperative learning in the secondary school: Maximizing language acquisition, academic achievement, and social development.* Washington, DC: National Clearinghouse for Bilingual Education.

Hudelson, S. (1994). Literacy development of second language children. In F. Genesee (Ed.), *Educating second language children* (pp. 129-158). Cambridge: Cambridge University Press.

Jacob, E., & Mattson, B. (1990). Cooperative learning: Instructing limited-English-proficient students in heterogeneous classes. In A.M. Padilla, H.H. Fairchild, C.M. Valadez (Eds.), *Bilingual education: Issues and strategies.* Newbury Park, CA: SAGE.

Jamieson, E.L., & Seaman, B. (1993). *America's immigrant challenge.* Time, 142(21), 3-9.

Johnson, D.M., & Roen, D.H. (Eds.). (1989). *Richness in writing: Empowering ESL students.* New York: Longman.

Johnson, D.W., & Johnson, R.T. (1986). *Circles of learning: Cooperation in the classroom.* Edina, MN: Interaction Book Company.

Johnson, D.W., Johnson, R.T., & Smith, K.A. (1991). *Active learning: Cooperation in the college classroom.* Edina, MN: Interaction Book Company.

Kagan, S. (1986). Cooperative learning and sociocultural factors in schooling. In *Beyond language: Social and cultural factors in schooling language minority students* (pp. 231-298). Sacramento, CA: California Department of Education.

Kagan, S. (1992). *Cooperative learning.* San Juan Capistrano, CA: Kagan Cooperative Learning.

Kloss, H. (1977). *The American bilingual tradition.* Cambridge, MA: Newbury House.

Krashen, S.D. (1977). Some issues relating to the Monitor Model. In H. Brown, C. Yorio & R. Crymes (Eds.), *On TESOL '77* (pp. 144-158). Washington, DC: Teachers of English to Speakers of Other Languages.

Krashen, S.D. (1981). *Second language acquisition and second language learning.* Oxford: Pergamon.

Krashen, S.D. (1982). *Principles and practices in second language acquisition.* Oxford: Pergamon.

Krashen, S.D. (1985). *The input hypothesis: Issues and implications.* New York: Longman.

Krashen, S.D., & Biber, D. (1988). *On course: Bilingual education's success in California.* Sacramento, CA: California Association for Bilingual Education.

Krashen, S.D., Scarcella, R.C., & Long, M.H. (Eds.). (1982). *Child-adult differences in second language acquisition.* Cambridge, MA: Newbury House.

Krashen, S.D., & Terrell, T.D. (1983). *The Natural Approach: Language acquisition in the classroom.* Oxford: Pergamon.

Lambert, W.E. (1975). Culture and language as factors in learning and education. In A. Wolfgang (Ed.), *Education of immigrant students.* Toronto: Ontario Institute for Studies in Education.

Lambert, W.E. (1984). An overview of issues in immersion education. In *Studies on immersion education: A collection for United States educators* (pp. 8-30). Sacramento, CA: California Department of Education.

Larsen-Freeman, D. (1985). Overview of theories of language learning and acquisition. In *Issues in English language development* (pp. 7-13). Washington, DC: National Clearinghouse for Bilingual Education.

Larsen-Freeman, D., & Long, M.H. (1991). *An introduction to second language acquisition research.* New York: Longman.

Lessow-Hurley, J. (1990). *The foundations of dual language instruction.* New York: Longman.

Lindholm, K.J. (1990). Bilingual immersion education: Criteria for program development. In A.M. Padilla, H.H. Fairchild & C.M. Valadez (Eds.), *Bilingual education: Issues and strategies* (pp. 91-105). Newbury Park, CA: SAGE.

Lindholm, K.J. (1991). Theoretical assumptions and empirical evidence for academic achievement in two languages. *Hispanic Journal of Behavioral Sciences,* 13, 3-17.

Lonergan, J. (1984). *Video in language teaching.* Cambridge: Cambridge University Press.

Long, M. (1988). Maturational constraints on language development. *Studies in Second Language Acquisition,* **12**, 251-285.

Lucas, T., Henze, R., & Donato, R. (1990). Promoting the success of latino language-minority students: An exploratory study of six high schools. *Harvard Educational Review,* 60, 315-340.

Malamah-Thomas, A. (1987). *Classroom interaction.* Oxford: Oxford University Press.

McCaleb, S.P. (1994). *Building communities of learners: A collaboration among teachers, students, families, and community.* New York: St. Martin's Press.

McKeon, D., & Malarz, L. (1991). *School-based management: What bilingual and ESL program directors should know.* Washington, DC: National Clearinghouse for Bilingual Education.

McLaughlin, B. (1984). *Second language acquisition in childhood: Vol. 1. Preschool children* (2nd ed.). Hillsdale, NJ: Lawrence Erlbaum.

McLaughlin, B. (1985). *Second language acquisition in childhood: Vol. 2. School-age children* (2nd ed.). Hillsdale, NJ: Lawrence Erlbaum.

McLaughlin, B. (1987). *Theories of second-language learning.* London: Arnold.

McLaughlin, B. (1992). *Myths and misconceptions about second language learning: What every teacher needs to unlearn.* Santa Cruz, CA: National Center for Research on Cultural Diversity and Second Language Learning.

Medina, M., Saldate, M., & Mishra, S. (1985). The sustaining effects of bilingual instruction: A follow-up study. *Journal of Instructional Psychology, 12*(3), 132-139.

Minicucci, C., & Olsen, L. (1992). *Programs for secondary limited English proficient students: A California study.* Washington, DC: National Clearinghouse for Bilingual Education.

Mohan, B.A. (1986). *Language and content.* Reading, MA: Addison-Wesley.

Moll, L.C., & Díaz, S. (1993). Change as the goal of educational research. In E. Jacob & C. Jordan (Eds.), *Minority education: Anthropological perspectives* (pp. 67-79). Norwood, NJ: Ablex.

Moll, L.C., Vélez-Ibáñez, C., Greenberg, J., & Rivera, C. (1990). *Community knowledge and classroom practice: Combining resources for literacy instruction.* Arlington, VA: Development Associates.

National Coalition of Advocates for Students. (1988). *New voices: Immigrant students in U.S. public schools.* Boston: Author.

National Coalition of Advocates for Students. (1991). *The good common school: Making the vision work for all children.* Boston: Author.

Oakes, J. (1985). *Keeping track: How schools structure inequality.* New Haven: Yale University Press.

Oakes, J. (1992). Can tracking research inform practice? Technical, normative, and political considerations. *Educational Researcher, 21*(4), 12-21.

Ogbu, J. (1974). *The next generation: An ethnography of education in an urban neighborhood.* New York: Academic Press.

Ogbu, J. (1978). *Minority education and caste: The American system in cross-cultural perspective.* New York: Academic Press.

Ogbu, J. (1987). Opportunity structure, cultural boundaries, and literacy. In J. Langer (Ed.), *Language, literacy, and culture: Issues of society and schooling.* Norwood, NJ: Ablex.

Ogbu, J. (1992). *Understanding cultural diversity.* Educational Researcher, 21(8), 5-24.

Ogbu, J. (1993). Variability in minority school performance: A problem in search of an explanation. In E. Jacob & C. Jordan (Eds.), *Minority education: Anthropological perspectives* (pp. 83-111). Norwood,NJ: Ablex.

Oller, J.W., Jr. (1993). *Methods that work: Ideas for literacy and language teachers* (2nd ed.). Boston: Heinle & Heinle.

O'Malley, J.M., & Chamot, A.U. (1990). *Learning strategies in second language acquisition.* Cambridge: Cambridge University Press.

O'Neil, J. (1993). Using technology to support 'authentic' learning. *ASCD Update, 35*(8), 1, 4-5.

Ovando, C.J. (1993). Language diversity and education. In J.A. Banks & C.A. Banks (Eds.), *Multicultural education: Issues and perspectives* (2nd ed., pp. 215-235). Boston: Allyn and Bacon.

Ovando, C.J., & Collier, V.P. (1995). *Bilingual and ESL classrooms: Teaching in multicultural contexts* (2nd ed.). New York: McGraw-Hill.

Oxford, R.L. (1990). *Language learning strategies: What every teacher should know.* Cambridge, MA: Newbury House.

Penfield, J. (1987). *The media: Catalysts for communicative language learning.* Reading, MA: Addison-Wesley.

Peyton, J.K. (Ed.). (1990). *Students and teachers writing together: Perspectives on journal writing.* Alexandria, VA: Teachers of English to Speakers of Other Languages.

Peyton, J.K., & Reed, L. (1990). *Dialogue journal writing with nonnative English speakers: A handbook for teachers.* Alexandria, VA: Teachers of English to Speakers of Other Languages.

Ramírez, J.D. (1992). Executive summary. *Bilingual Research Journal, 16*(1-2), 1-62.

Richard-Amato, P. (1988). *Making it happen: Interaction in the second language classroom.* New York: Longman.

Richard-Amato, P.A., & Snow, M.A. (Eds.). (1992). *The multicultural classroom: Readings for content-area teachers.* New York: Longman.

Rigg, P., & Enright, D.S. (Eds.). (1986). *Children and ESL: Integrating perspectives.* Alexandria, VA: Teachers of English to Speakers of Other Languages.

Rivera, C., & Zehler, A. (1990). *Collaboration in teaching and learning: Findings from the Innovative Approaches Research Project.* Arlington, VA: Development Associates.

Rosebery, A.S., Warren, B., & Conant, F.R. (1992). *Appropriating scientific discourse: Findings from language minority classrooms.* Santa Cruz, CA: National Center for Research on Cultural Diversity and Second Language Learning.

Rosier, P., & Holm, W. (1980). *The Rock Point experience: A longitudinal study of a Navajo school program.* Washington, DC: Center for Applied Linguistics.

Rothman, R. (1991). Schools stress speeding up, not slowing down. *Education Week,* 11(9), 1, 14-15.

Samway, K.D. (1992). *Writers' workshop and children acquiring English as a non-native language.* Washington, DC: National Clearinghouse for Bilingual Education.

Saunders, G. (1988). *Bilingual children: From birth to teens.* Clevedon, England: Multilingual Matters.

Saville-Troike, M. (1984). What really matters in second language learning for academic achievement? *TESOL Quarterly,* 18, 199-219.

Scarcella, R. (1990). *Teaching language minority students in the multicultural classroom.* Englewood Cliffs, NJ: Prentice Hall Regents.

Scarcella, R.C., & Oxford, R.L. (1992). *The tapestry of language learning: The individual in the communicative classroom.* Boston: Heinle & Heinle.

Schumann, J. (1978). The acculturation model for second language acquisition. In R. Gingras (Ed.), *Second language acquisition and foreign language teaching* (pp. 27-50). Washington, DC: Center for Applied Linguistics.

Scovel, T. (1988). *A time to speak: A psycholinguistic inquiry into the critical period for human speech.* Cambridge, MA: Newbury House.

Sharry, F. (1994). *The rise of nativism in the United States and how to respond to it.* Washington, DC: The National Immigration Forum.

Shoemaker, C.L., & Shoemaker, F.F. (1991). *Interactive techniques for the ESL classroom.* Boston: Heinle & Heinle.

Shor, I., & Freire, P. (1987). *A pedagogy for liberation: Dialogues on transforming education.* New York: Bergin & Garvey.

Short, D.J. (1991). *How to integrate language and content instruction: A training manual* (2nd ed.). Washington, DC: Center for Applied Linguistics.

Skutnabb-Kangas, T. (1981). *Bilingualism or not: The education of minorities.* Philadelphia: Multilingual Matters.

Skutnabb-Kangas, T., & Cummins, J. (Eds.). (1988). *Minority education: From shame to struggle.* Clevedon, England: Multilingual Matters.

Slavin, R.E. (Ed.). (1988). *School and classroom organization.* Hillsdale, NJ: Erlbaum.

Smallwood, B.A. (1991). *The literature connection: A read-aloud guide for multicultural classrooms.* Reading, MA: Addison-Wesley.

Smallwood, B.A. (1992). *Input or interaction: Which strategies contribute to second language acquisition in elementary literature-based classrooms?* Unpublished manuscript, Center for Bilingual/Multicultural/ESL Education, George Mason University, Fairfax, VA.

Snow, C.E. (1990). Rationales for native language instruction: Evidence from research. In A.M. Padilla, H.H. Fairchild, & C.M. Valadez (Eds.), *Bilingual education: Issues and strategies.* Newbury Park, CA: Sage.

Snow, C.E., & Ferguson, C.A. (Eds.). (1977). *Talking to children: Language input and acquisition.* Cambridge: Cambridge University Press.

Solís, A. (1989). Use of the Natural Approach Teaching Model: Application of second language acquisition research by teachers of limited-English-proficient students (Doctoral dissertation, George Mason University). *Dissertation Abstracts International.*

Spener, D. (1988). Transitional bilingual education and the socialization of immigrants. *Harvard Educational Review,* 58, 133-153.

Stern, H.H. (1963). *Foreign languages in primary education: The teaching of foreign or second languages to younger children.* Hamburg: International Studies in Education, UNESCO Institute for Education.

Stewart, D.W. (1993). *Immigration and education: The crisis and the opportunities.* New York: Macmillan.

Suárez-Orozco, M.M. (1987). Towards a psychosocial understanding of Hispanic adaptation to American schooling. In H.T. Trueba (Ed.), *Success or failure? Learning and the language minority student* (pp. 156-168). Cambridge, MA: Newbury House.

Suárez-Orozco, M.M. (1993). "Becoming somebody": Central American immigrants in U.S. inner-city schools. In E. Jacob & C. Jordan (Eds.), *Minority education: Anthropological perspectives* (pp. 129-143). Norwood, NJ: Ablex.

Susser, B. (1993). ESL/EFL process writing with computers. *CAELL Journal,* 4(2), 16-22.

Swain, M. (1981). Time and timing in bilingual education. *Language Learning,* 31, 1-15.

Swain, M. (1985). Communicative competence: Some roles of comprehensible input and comprehensible output in its development. In S. Gass & C. Madden (Eds.), *Input in second language acquisition* (pp. 235-253). Cambridge, MA: Newbury House.

Swain, M., & Lapkin, S. (1981). *Bilingual education in Ontario: A decade of research.* Toronto: Ontario Institute for Studies in Education.

Swain, M., Lapkin, S., Rowen, N., & Hart, D. (1990). The role of mother tongue literacy in third language learning. Language, *Culture and Curriculum,* 3, 65-81.

Terrell, T.D. (1981). The Natural Approach in bilingual education. In *Schooling and language minority students* (pp. 117-146). Sacramento, CA: California Department of Education.

Tharp, R.G., & Gallimore, R. (1988). *Rousing minds to life: Teaching, learning, and schooling in social context.* Cambridge: Cambridge University Press.

Tharp, R.G., & Yamauchi, L.A. (1994). *Effective instructional conversation in Native American classrooms.* Santa Cruz, CA: National Center for Research on Cultural Diversity and Second Language Learning.

Thomas, W.P. (1992). An analysis of the research methodology of the Ramírez study. *Bilingual Research Journal,* 16(1-2), 213-245.

Thomas, W.P. (1994). *The Cognitive Academic Language Learning Approach Project for Mathematics.* Manuscript submitted for publication.

Thomas, W.P., & Collier, V.P. (1995). *Language minority student achievement and program effectiveness.* Washington, D.C.: National Clearinghouse for Bilingual Education.

Thonis, E. (1981). Reading instruction for language minority students. In *Schooling and language minority students* (pp. 147-181). Sacramento, CA: California Department of Education.

Tikunoff, W., Ward, B., van Broekhuizen, D., Romero, M., Castañeda, L., Lucas, T., & Katz, A. (1991). *Final report: A descriptive study of significant features of exemplary special alternative instructional programs.* Los Alamitos, CA: Southwest Regional Educational Laboratory.

Tinajero, J.V., & Ada, A.F. (Eds.). (1993). *The power of two languages: Literacy and biliteracy for Spanish-speaking students.* New York: Macmillan/McGraw-Hill.

Trueba, H.T. (1991). The role of culture in bilingual instruction: Linking linguistic and cognitive development to cultural knowledge. In Ofelia García (Ed.), *Bilingual education* (pp. 43-55). Amsterdam: John Benjamins.

Trueba, H.T., Guthrie, G.P., & Au, K.H. (Eds.). (1981). *Culture and the bilingual classroom: Studies in classroom ethnography.* Cambridge, MA: Newbury House.

Trueba, H.T., Jacobs, L., & Kirton, E. (1990). *Cultural conflict and adaptation: The case of Hmong children in American society.* New York: Falmer Press.

Tyack, D.B. (1974). *The one best system: A history of American urban education.* Cambridge, MA: Harvard University Press.

Valdez Pierce, L. (1991). *Effective schools for language minority students.* Washington, DC: The Mid-Atlantic Equity Center.

Veltman, C. (1988). *The future of the Spanish language in the United States.* Washington, DC: Hispanic Policy Development Project.

Vogt, L.A., Jordan, C., & Tharp, R.G. (1993). Explaining school failure, producing school success: Two cases. In E. Jacob & C. Jordan (Eds.), *Minority education: Anthropological perspectives* (pp. 53-65). Norwood, NJ: Ablex.

Vygotsky, L.S. (1962). *Thought and language.* Cambridge, MA: Harvard University Press.

Vygotsky, L.S. (1978). *Mind in society.* Cambridge, MA: Harvard University Press.

Warren, B., Rosebery, A.S., & Conant, F. (1990). *Cheche konnen: Collaborative scientific inquiry in language minority classrooms.* Arlington, VA: Development Associates.

Wells, G. (1985). *Language development in the pre-school years.* Cambridge: Cambridge University Press.

Wheelock, A. (1992). *Crossing the tracks: How "untracking" can save America's schools.* New York: The New Press.

Williams, J.D., & Snipper, G.C. (1990). *Literacy and bilingualism.* New York: Longman.

Wolfram, W., & Christian, D. (1989). *Dialects and education: Issues and answers.* Englewood Cliffs, NJ: Prentice Hall Regents.

Wong Fillmore, L. (1985). Second language learning in children: A proposed model. In *Issues in English language development* (pp. 33-42). Washington, DC: National Clearinghouse for Bilingual Education.

Wong Fillmore, L. (1989). Teachability and second language acquisition. In R. Schiefelbusch & M. Rice (Eds.), *The teachability of language* (pp. 311-332). Baltimore, MD: Paul Brookes.

Wong Fillmore, L. (1991a). A question for early-childhood programs: English first or families first? *Education Week,* June 19, 1991.

Wong Fillmore, L. (1991b). Second language learning in children: A model of language learning isocial context. In E. Bialystok (Ed.), *Language processing in bilingual children* (pp. 49-69). Cambridge: Cambridge University Press

Wong Fillmore, L. , & Valadez, C. (1986). Teaching bilingual learners. In M.C. Wittrock (Ed.), *Handbook of research on teaching* (3rd ed., pp. 648-685). New York: Macmillan.